First World War
and Army of Occupation
War Diary
France, Belgium and Germany

49 DIVISION
Divisional Troops
Royal Army Veterinary Corps
1/1 West Riding Veterinary Section
16 April 1915 - 28 March 1919

WO95/2791/1

The Naval & Military Press Ltd
www.nmarchive.com
Published in association with The National Archives

Published by

The Naval & Military Press Ltd

Unit 10 Ridgewood Industrial Park,

Uckfield, East Sussex,

TN22 5QE England

Tel: +44 (0) 1825 749494

www.naval-military-press.com

www.nmarchive.com

This diary has been reprinted in facsimile from the original. Any imperfections are inevitably reproduced and the quality may fall short of modern type and cartographic standards.

© Crown Copyright
Images reproduced by permission of The National Archives, London, England, 2015.

Contents

Document type	Place/Title	Date From	Date To
Heading	WO95/2791/1		
Heading	49th Division Mobile Vety Secn. Apr 1915-Mar 1919		
Heading	49th Division W.R. Mobile Vety Section Vol I 16.4-5.7.15.		
War Diary	Doncaster	16/04/1915	16/04/1915
War Diary	Southampton	16/04/1915	16/04/1915
War Diary	Harve	17/04/1915	17/04/1915
War Diary	Berequette	18/04/1915	18/04/1915
War Diary	Gaurbecque	19/04/1915	19/04/1915
War Diary	Merville	21/04/1915	29/04/1915
War Diary	Merville	22/04/1915	12/05/1915
War Diary	Estaires	14/05/1915	24/05/1915
War Diary		23/05/1915	23/05/1915
War Diary	Estaires	26/05/1915	05/06/1915
War Diary		03/06/1915	09/06/1915
War Diary	Estaires	10/06/1915	10/06/1915
War Diary	Grand Mortier	11/06/1915	14/06/1915
War Diary	Estaires	14/06/1915	14/06/1915
War Diary	Grand Mother	17/06/1915	19/06/1915
War Diary		16/06/1915	19/06/1915
War Diary	Sheet 36 G. 10. 8.8. Grand Mortier	20/06/1915	21/06/1915
War Diary	Brice Rides	23/06/1915	26/06/1915
War Diary	Move	01/07/1915	01/07/1915
War Diary	Castre	01/07/1915	20/07/1915
War Diary	Watou	04/07/1915	05/07/1915
Heading	49th Division 49th Mobile Vety Section Vol II 6-7-8-8-15		
War Diary	Watou	06/07/1915	09/07/1915
War Diary	On The Move	09/07/1915	09/07/1915
War Diary	Poperinghe	10/07/1915	24/07/1915
War Diary	Poperinghe	20/07/1915	06/08/1915
War Diary	Poperinghe	05/08/1915	08/08/1915
War Diary	A.G. G.H.Q. 3rd Echelon The Base	09/08/1915	09/08/1915
Heading	49th Division 49th Mobile Vety Section Vol III 10-27th August 1915		
War Diary	N Poperinghe	10/08/1915	15/08/1915
War Diary	N Poperinghe	13/08/1915	17/08/1915
War Diary	N Poperinghe	15/08/1915	28/08/1915
War Diary		27/08/1915	27/08/1915
Heading	49th Division 49th Mobile Vety Section Vol IV Sept 15		
War Diary	Poperinghe	02/09/1915	09/09/1915
War Diary		06/09/1915	11/09/1915
War Diary	N Poperinghe	09/09/1915	09/09/1915
War Diary		07/09/1915	18/09/1915
War Diary		13/09/1915	29/09/1915
War Diary		23/09/1915	23/09/1915
Heading	49th Division 49th (W R) Mobile Vety Section Vol V Oct 15		
War Diary	In The Field	01/10/1915	06/10/1915
War Diary		05/10/1915	07/10/1915

War Diary		05/10/1915	09/10/1915
War Diary		08/10/1915	11/10/1915
War Diary	In The Field	13/10/1915	16/10/1915
War Diary		11/10/1915	11/10/1915
War Diary	In The Field	17/10/1915	17/10/1915
War Diary		16/10/1915	18/10/1915
War Diary		16/10/1915	26/10/1915
War Diary		25/10/1915	25/10/1915
War Diary	In The Field	24/10/1915	31/10/1915
War Diary	49th Division 49th Mob. Vet: Sec Nov 1915 Vol VI		
War Diary	In The Field	01/11/1915	04/11/1915
War Diary	In The Field	03/11/1915	04/11/1915
War Diary	In The Field	03/11/1915	08/11/1915
War Diary	In The Field	05/11/1915	05/11/1915
War Diary	In The Field	02/11/1915	11/11/1915
War Diary	In The Field	10/11/1915	10/11/1915
War Diary	In The Field	08/11/1915	29/11/1915
Heading	49th Mob. Vet. Sec Dec Vol VII		
War Diary	In The Field	01/12/1915	09/12/1915
War Diary	In The Field	08/12/1915	21/12/1915
War Diary	In The Field	19/12/1915	30/12/1915
War Diary	In The Field	29/12/1915	30/12/1915
War Diary	In The Field	29/12/1915	29/12/1915
Heading	49th Div Mob Vet. Sec. Jan 1916 Vol VIII		
War Diary	In The Field	01/01/1916	01/01/1916
War Diary	Ledringham	03/01/1916	03/01/1916
War Diary		02/01/1916	02/01/1916
War Diary	In The Field	07/01/1916	24/01/1916
War Diary	In The Field	23/01/1916	31/01/1916
War Diary	In The Field	28/01/1916	31/01/1916
Heading	1/1 W.R. Mob Vety Sec Vol IX		
War Diary	In The Field	02/02/1916	23/02/1916
War Diary	In The Field	22/02/1916	22/02/1916
War Diary	In The Field	20/02/1916	24/02/1916
War Diary	In The Field	23/02/1916	29/02/1916
Heading	1/1 W.R. Mob Vety Sec Vol X		
War Diary	In The Field	02/03/1916	06/03/1916
War Diary	In The Field	04/03/1916	10/03/1916
War Diary	In The Field	08/03/1916	31/03/1916
Heading	Mob Vety Sect Vol XI		
War Diary	In The Field	03/04/1916	19/04/1916
War Diary	In The Field	01/04/1916	17/04/1916
War Diary	In The Field	14/04/1916	25/04/1916
War Diary	In The Field	24/04/1916	18/05/1916
War Diary	In The Field	17/05/1916	05/06/1916
War Diary	In The Field	03/06/1916	12/06/1916
War Diary	In The Field	08/06/1916	19/06/1916
War Diary	In The Field	07/06/1916	28/06/1916
War Diary		25/06/1916	27/06/1916
War Diary	In The Field	18/06/1916	30/06/1916
War Diary		29/06/1916	29/06/1916
Heading		28/06/1916	28/06/1916
War Diary	In The Field	30/06/1916	30/06/1916
Heading	A.G. G.H.Z. 39 Echelon The Base	04/08/1916	04/08/1916
War Diary	In The Field	01/07/1916	16/08/1916
War Diary		15/08/1916	23/08/1916

War Diary	In The Field	24/08/1916	13/09/1916
War Diary	In The Field	12/09/1916	19/09/1916
War Diary	In The Field	18/09/1916	18/09/1916
War Diary	In The Field	14/09/1916	30/09/1916
Miscellaneous	Headquarters 49th (WR) Division	02/11/1916	02/11/1916
War Diary	In The Field	01/10/1916	12/10/1916
War Diary	In The Field	12/10/1916	25/11/1916
War Diary	In The Field	23/11/1916	30/11/1916
Heading	War Diary Of 1/1st (W.R.) Mobile Veterinary Section For December 1916 Vol 19		
War Diary	In The Field	02/12/1916	10/12/1916
War Diary	In The Field	09/12/1916	21/12/1916
War Diary	In The Field	20/12/1916	30/12/1916
Heading	War Diary Of Mobile Vet Sect 49th (WR) Division For January 1917 Vol 20		
War Diary	In The Field	01/01/1917	31/01/1917
War Diary	In The Field	30/01/1917	30/01/1917
Heading	War Diary Of For 1917.		
Heading	War Diary Of 1/1st (W.R.) Mobile Veterinary Sect For February 1917. Vol 21		
War Diary	In The Field	01/02/1917	03/02/1917
War Diary	In The Field	02/02/1917	04/02/1917
War Diary	In The Field	03/02/1917	28/02/1917
Heading	War Diary Of 1/1st (WR) Mobile Veterinary Section For March 1917 Vol 21		
War Diary	In The Field	01/03/1917	21/03/1917
War Diary	In The Field	20/03/1917	22/03/1917
War Diary	In The Field	21/03/1917	30/03/1917
Heading	War Diary Of 49th (WR) Div Mobile Vety Section For April 1917 Vol 22		
War Diary	In The Field	02/04/1917	02/04/1917
War Diary	In The Field	01/04/1917	28/04/1917
War Diary	In The Field	27/04/1917	30/04/1917
War Diary	In The Field	29/04/1917	29/04/1917
War Diary	In The Field	28/04/1917	30/05/1917
War Diary	In The Field	29/05/1917	29/05/1917
War Diary	In The Field	13/05/1917	31/05/1917
Heading	War Diary Of 1/1st (WR) Mob Vet Sect For June 1917 Vol 24		
War Diary	In The Field	01/06/1917	05/06/1917
War Diary		25/05/1917	12/06/1917
War Diary	In The Field	06/06/1917	24/06/1917
War Diary	In The Field	13/06/1917	23/06/1917
War Diary	In The Field	22/06/1917	30/06/1917
Heading	War Diary Of 1/1st W.R. Mob Vet Set For July 1917		
War Diary	In The Field	01/07/1917	10/07/1917
War Diary	In The Field	09/07/1917	31/07/1917
Heading	War Diary Of 1/1st WR Mob Vet Sect For August 1917 Vol 26		
War Diary	In The Field	03/08/1917	27/08/1917
War Diary	In The Field	23/08/1917	30/08/1917
Heading	War Diary of 1/1st (W.R) Mob Vet Sect For September 1917 Vol 27		
War Diary	In The Field	04/09/1917	29/09/1917
Heading	War Diary of 1/1st W.R. Mobile Vet Section For 1st to 31st October 1917 Vol 28		

Heading	H.Q. 49 (W R) Division Through D A D V S	31/10/1917	31/10/1917
War Diary	In The Field	01/10/1917	22/10/1917
War Diary	In The Field	21/10/1917	26/10/1917
War Diary	In The Field	25/10/1917	30/10/1917
Heading	War Diary of 1/1st W.R Mob Vet Sect For November 1917 Vol 29		
War Diary	In The Field	03/11/1917	12/11/1917
War Diary	In The Field	10/11/1917	26/11/1917
War Diary	In The Field	18/11/1917	30/11/1917
Heading	War Diary 1/1 W.R. Mob Vet Sect January 18 Vol 31		
War Diary		02/01/1918	31/01/1918
War Diary	War Diary of 1/1 West Riding Mob Vet Sect for February 1918 Vol 32		
War Diary	Field	01/02/1918	28/02/1918
Heading	War Diary of 1/1 (W.R.) M.V.S 49 Division For The Month of March 1918 Vol 33		
War Diary	In The Field	02/03/1918	03/03/1918
War Diary	In The Field	01/03/1918	29/03/1918
Heading	War Diary Of 1/1st (W.R.) Mob Vet Sec: For Month Of April 1918 Vol 34		
War Diary	In The Field	03/04/1918	30/04/1918
War Diary	War Diary of 1/1 (W.R) Mob Vet Sect For May 1918 Vol 35		
War Diary	In The Field	01/05/1918	20/05/1918
War Diary		18/05/1918	31/05/1918
Heading	War Diary of 1/1 (WR) M.V.S. 49 (WR) Division For The Month of June 1918 Vol 36		
War Diary	In The Field	01/06/1918	30/06/1918
Heading	In The Field	26/06/1918	26/06/1918
Heading	War Diary of 1/1 (WR) M.V.S For The Month of July 1918 Vol 37		
War Diary	In The Field	01/07/1918	07/07/1918
War Diary	In The Field	05/07/1918	24/07/1918
War Diary	In The Field	22/07/1918	30/07/1918
Heading	War Diary of 1/1 (W R) M.V.S. 49 (WR) Division For The Month of August 1918 Vol 38		
War Diary	In The Field	02/08/1918	14/08/1918
War Diary	In The Field	10/08/1918	31/08/1918
Heading	War Diary of 1/1st (W R) M.V.S 49th West Riding) Division For The Month of September 1918 Vol 39		
War Diary	In The Field	01/09/1918	25/09/1918
War Diary	In The Field	23/09/1918	30/09/1918
Heading	War Diary of 1/1 (W R) M.V.S. For The Month of October 1918 Vol 41		
War Diary		01/10/1918	31/10/1918
Heading	War Diary of 1/1 (W R) M.V.S for The Month of November 1918 Vol 42		
War Diary	In The Field	01/11/1918	30/11/1918
Miscellaneous	H.Q. 49 (WR) Division	04/01/1919	04/01/1919
War Diary	In The Field	01/12/1918	27/12/1918
War Diary	In The Field	26/12/1918	31/12/1918
Heading	War Diary of 49th Bn M.G. Corps January 1919 Vol II		
War Diary	In The Field	01/01/1919	17/01/1919
War Diary	In The Field	15/01/1919	31/01/1919
War Diary	War Diary of 1/1 (WR) M.V.S. For The Month of February 1919 Vol 45		

War Diary		01/02/1919	28/02/1919
Miscellaneous	H Q Q 49 Div	05/04/1919	05/04/1919
War Diary	In The Field	01/03/1919	28/03/1919

WO 05/27091/1

49TH DIVISION

MOBILE VETY SECN.
APR 1915-MAR 1919

49TH DIVISION

121/6023

aVD

49th Division

W.R. mobility return

Vol I 16.4 — 5.7.15.

Army Form C. 2118.

WAR DIARY
or
INTELLIGENCE SUMMARY.
(Erase heading not required.)

Instructions regarding War Diaries and Intelligence Summaries are contained in F. S. Regs., Part II. and the Staff Manual respectively. Title pages will be prepared in manuscript.

Place	Date	Hour	Summary of Events and Information	Remarks and references to Appendices
Doncaster	16-4-15	3.25 a.m.	Entrained at Shakespeare Dock	
Southampton	"	4.45 a.m.	Detrained	
"	"	6 p.m.	Embarked on S.S. Architect	
Havre	17-4-15	10 a.m.	Disembarked	
"	"	11 p.m.	Entrained at Gare Maritime. Returned to include 21-4-15	
Busigneule	18-4-15 12 Midt		Detrained - at 2 a.m. on the 19th inst. Marched off & arrived Lusbecque about 4 a.m. that day.	
Lambrecque	19-4-15 2.30 p.m.		Marched off through St. Venant & arrived at Merville	
Merville	21-4-15 9.30 p.m.		Great Rations for 22-4-15 & made out rolls for 8 days in front.	
	24-4-15 2.30 p.m.		Entrained a Batch of Horses (Sick) for Headquarters 5th Infantry Division & St. Bulford	
	26-4-15 2.30 p.m.		Entrained 19 Sick Horses under Sept Yates 12th Buffords. Baker & Lilly. Singleton, Duffown v Baker.	
"	29-4-15	"	"	
"	1-5-15	-	Pte G. Lewis Executed	
"	2-4-15 6 p.m.		P. S. of Lewis, Lilly, Duffown around Two Asylums 20 miles away.	
	6-5-15 2.30 p.m.		Entrained at La Gorgue Station for Merville for a Batch of 10 Horses for depot ground	

J. Eckon Q.M.S.

WAR DIARY
or
INTELLIGENCE SUMMARY.

(Erase heading not required.)

Army Form C. 2118.

Instructions regarding War Diaries and Intelligence Summaries are contained in F. S. Regs., Part II. and the Staff Manual respectively. Title pages will be prepared in manuscript.

Place	Date	Hour	Summary of Events and Information	Remarks and references to Appendices
Merville	11-5-15	3.30 p.m.	Entrained at La Gorgue Station a Batch of 8 Horses for Abbeville the Staff Journeyed	
	12-5-15	2 p.m.	Marched off to Calais arriving there at 4 p.m.	
Calais	14-5-15	11 a.m.	C/No 20 Pte J. Batty A.V.C. arrived from Remt. Station for duty = posted in orders	
"	"	3 p.m.	Two Horses in Lon.l entrained at La Gorgue Station the Sergt. Baker	
	15-5-15	3 p.m.	Eleven Horses entrained at La Gorgue (two Horses in Lon.l) for Base	
	17-5-15		Sergt. Baker returned from Base with Horse	
	20-5-15		After having been able to Form a Horse Ambulance I returned the same on my tour. The news to day removed it so he needed it urgently. This Ambulance has been of great assistance to me, I consider it strong enough that the Government ought to allow one on the Establishment of the Mobile Veterinary Section. R. Nor-with Lce/Cpl at foot was taken over from 1st Battery H.M. led R.F.A. Lilly Lc/Cpl. Lcon R. Wapping have been hereof about 4 mile from my line.	
Calais	21-5-15	8.34 p.m.	Started 9 Horses v 1 Lon.l to Abbeville to hospital gate.	
	23-5-15		Private G. Cooke returned to duty from No 6 Veterinary Hospital	

WAR DIARY
or
INTELLIGENCE SUMMARY

Army Form C. 2118.

(Erase heading not required.)

Place	Date	Hour	Summary of Events and Information	Remarks and references to Appendices
Estaires	26-5-15	8.30 a.m.	Summoned before General Bullock - Subsequently under shell fire near Rouge Selent.	
			Same date Corporal Yates when fetching straw from the same place reports that shell fire is heavier.	
	27-5-15	9.30 a.m.	Court of Enquiry re alleged.	
	31-5-15	3.30 p.m.	10 Horses 2 Mules 1 Foal entrained at La Gorgue & sent to Base.	
	28-5-15		Summoned before General Bullock 9.20 a.m. Incident closed.	
	3/6/15		Drugs received from advanced depôt of Vet. Base. Units notified.	
	5-6-15		3 Lots of Veterinary Stores left. Units concerned again notified.	
	3-6-15	3 p.m.	General Bullock visited Lines.	
	6-6-15		11 Horses 1 Mange & Suspect of Mange entrained at La Gorgue dispatched to Base. Lt/ Sergt. Greenwood. Pte Bafford & Tatner. (Corporal Ingleton)	
	7-6-15	3.30 p.m.	7 Horses & 4 Mules sent to Base. (Poss. Mange Horses.)	
	9-6-15		12 Horses 1 Mule sent to Base.	
			9 Horses	

R.M.T

Army Form C. 2118.

WAR DIARY
or
INTELLIGENCE SUMMARY.
(Erase heading not required.)

Place	Date	Hour	Summary of Events and Information	Remarks and references to Appendices
Calais	10-6-15	9.20 a.m.	Marched off from Calais to Grand Mortin - Halt at G.10 a.S.S.	
Grand Mortin	11-6-15	7 A.m.	Went to Steenwerk to get a Halt - (Harrard)	
"	14=8=15	5=20	Entrained 8 Horses = 2 Mules - A Mart - Ford to the base mules	
			Sergt. L. Baker Pte A.B. Sykes shewed great pluck in driving away Horses from the Lad & saved the Lad being sunked into the river.	
Calais			Monsieur Guinaud removed from his appointment. Monsieur Dubois = attached instead	
Grand Mortin	17=6-15	3-30	Entrained at La Gorgue Two change bases. 10 Mare 7 foal & Seventeen Horses.	
	15-6-15		Made agreement with Monsieur Wallette fervour in lieu of that approved by A.D. of V.S. Horslet, Horse 7, 1 Mule in different places. Loaded 2 Horses in the Morning 7, 1 at night to La Gorgue Station	
"	16-6-15		8 Horses to La Gorgue Station	
	19-6-15		Sergt. Guinaud Pte Horton Monleo, Taylor, Bedford, Lambert returned with Horses (Gun 14 Masta)	

O.M.F.

WAR DIARY or INTELLIGENCE SUMMARY

Army Form C. 2118.

Place	Date	Hour	Summary of Events and Information	Remarks and references to Appendices
Huts 3 & 9, 1° A.F.B.			Orders to move	
Grand Morlies	20-8-15			
	21-8-15	8:00 am	Marched off & proceeded to Bruie Kislea Huts 26 of 1.C.1.7.7. Good billets and his small field Marge & Inspected Marge in a field in another farm	
Bruie Rules	23-8-15	3 pm	Seventeen Horses sent to Boe it. Corporal Singleton.	
	25-8-15	5 pm	Eighteen Horses Mule sent to the Base & Thirry Smith Marking.	
Mon	1/7/15	9 am	Marched off from Bruie Rielo & Marched to Laotie, that other events of the Division having already moved off from this area. Picket of a Horse belonging to 2nd Field Ambulance at Joulie & left a Horse i/c of the Maire belonging to 3rd (L.R.) B.R.F.A.	
Laotie	Night of 1-7/15		Billeted at a farm close to Laotie.	
	2-7/15		Marched from Laotie to Water & Reported arrival to H.Q. 48th Infantry Bde. since this move was carried out under their orders. Also reported arrival to A.D.V.S.	

WAR DIARY
or
INTELLIGENCE SUMMARY.

(Erase heading not required.)

Army Form C. 2118.

Place	Date	Hour	Summary of Events and Information	Remarks and references to Appendices
Watou	4/7/15		For the March it was absolutely necessary to transit a wagon to improve horses & ran received sore (horses) Mark was quite satisfactory. Wagon returned in charge of Corporal Saughton. Went to Locatie. Visited Horse left there & (2) R.B.H.A. afin off stock – dressed handaged & left arranged with Lt R.D. in returning Horses for the boat. During my absence at Locatie D.D.V.S. & A.D. V.S. visited Lieut Potts advising me arrived too late, got it at 4 p.m. on returning from Locatie.	
	5/7/15		The need of additional Stores not so importance. One Wagon field is taken up by Rations & forage absolutely. The remaining wagon totally inadequate to take the Stores, Office Stationery etc. together with the tents & protect it at the stores. Corporal Saughton returned with his wagon on to the town. at 9 a.m. & brought him on to the town, H.D.V.S. visited & instructed Horses – Mule & No N. Br. fld tested with Mallon at 5 p.m.	

1577 Wt.W10791/1773 500,000 1/15 D.D.&L. A.D.S.S./Forms/C. 2118.

121/5401

49th Division

29th Mobile Vety Section

Vol III

6-7-8-9-15

A.Q.(W.R) Mobile Veterinary Section

Army Form C. 2118.

WAR DIARY
or
INTELLIGENCE SUMMARY.
(Erase heading not required.)

Place	Date	Hour	Summary of Events and Information	Remarks and references to Appendices
Watou	6/4/15	9a—	Ten Horses Mules taken to Godwaersvelde Station for entrainment to Boulogne. What horse from Doulieu had to be shot at Godwaersvelde for deformed fracture off Radius — Fracture only became evident on arrival there — Mules trained to Pradeseyne, Stakeover carcass — Animal was separated from Mules to Godwaersvelde. Sheep P.M. Mare was noted from Baas late to Station — Two horses (Suspicious Mange) embarked for base to Sergt. Greenwood — P. Hopes at Proven — New to Unit even A. 2.B. (Shoot 28) designated of Unit Hg (W.R.) Mobile Veterinary Section 1 Blanket per man to be returned.	
"	4/4/15	6a		
"	"	2p	Through Payers he to their billets area — Inspected 3 farmer reported to Headquarters	
"	"	"	Head vegimet for horses in fact there is scarcely a day passes by that a foot is required to my to lead mare dogs call called — very unfortunate episode on it.	
	9/4/15	1p	Nine Horses Three Mules entrained at Godwaersvelde for the disposal. Moved off from line for 2 p.m. Arrived at New Station beyond Poperinghe	

WAR DIARY or INTELLIGENCE SUMMARY

Army Form C. 2118.

Place	Date	Hour	Summary of Events and Information	Remarks and references to Appendices
On Kalhari	9/4/15			
Wanjerike	10/4/15	9 a.m.	about 6 p.m. 20.A.D.10.4. Sheet 28 - Borrowed wagon & more. Proceeded to field & collected horse reported by Colonel Wilson. Wanjerike collected 4 tarno mules & belonging to Lt Col Wilson's Divisional Amm. Column - also collected a horse belonging to 1st Co. R.B. 13 R.F.A.	
"	13/4/15	"	Drove Murrell & ghost horse returned to 53 W.R.F. Amt. Thompson & Black Mare " 3rd W.R.F. Amt.	
"	14 "	11 "	Colonel Wilson inspected lines " Par Parade	
"	14/4/15	"	19 Horses 3 Mules sent to Engr Greenwood - Two cases of Mange.	
"	15/4/15	"	Supplies.	
"	"	"	Moved into next billet past the Muchlangal - to Sheet 24 T 12 E 3.10.	
"	22/4/15	"	Proceeded to lines of North Riding Horse Battery & inspected horses & Mules Lieut-Colonel Wilson & Major Kerr & Holder Whitehead they present - 70 R Capt Bailey with switch - Inspected & observed the India - Army hospital & method of malleinization & also ammunition for Agar field Hospital Farm (the Horse Battery) - Amm & Harness.	
	23/4/15			

WAR DIARY
or
INTELLIGENCE SUMMARY

Army Form C. 2118.

Place	Date	Hour	Summary of Events and Information	Remarks and references to Appendices
Pitlochry	24/7/15		6" Mobile Section - whole Unit. Hotchkiss gave a demonstration of Intra tarsal & pubertal Method of Mallein isation. Edgar Horses 1 Mule sent to race if Corporal Yates. V. Hospital Horse. Two B.M.R. Horses noted with Neck rays destroyed. P.M. Exam - Slothed Glanders Nodules present in Lungs cad Liver + charging in one case. Another Mucous Membrane Plaques open but Abnormal Velvet pile pleury in each lung also the CR Lymphs present on live. - Pte Butter to report to Persons M. Lutory left to take over appointment of S.S.M. Corporal Yates Casey of Staff Veterinary Corps - Pay herds to 28.7.15. Rapidly practice in Hygiene - Pte Butter to report	
" "	26/7/15		To Gen Hospital.	
" "	26/7/15		1020 7 M allein armed.	
	28/7/15		Pte Butler proceeded on leave to England 28/7/15 to 4-8-15	
	31/7/15		J Moore horses rated from Pokersby to Bazi Via Grange	
" "	1/8/15		Sergt Greenwood detailed to relieve L.G. Hartley 147 Infantry Brigade	

WAR DIARY
or
INTELLIGENCE SUMMARY.

Army Form C. 2118.

Place	Date	Hour	Summary of Events and Information	Remarks and references to Appendices
Poperinghe	4/6/15		Colonel Fowler reported to have come to the M.K. lines -	
"	5/6/15		Fourteen cases of Mules sailed to Base today - 4 cases Mange included.	
"			Mr Butler attended sick hors from 11.45am 5/6/15.	
"			Ples Hopkins, Furey + Beeched on leave 6 days 5/6/15.	
"	5/6/15		Ple Butler's explanation Mile landing officer at Boulogne directed him to return to Butler's explanation Mile landing officer at Boulogne directed him to return thereon the am of 4/6/15.	
"	6/6/15		Sergt Carrick attended 3 days confinement to lines Be extra guards for neglect of duty (allowing horses to get away with danger to the horse transport horses).	
"	5/6/15		M.Mrss 1162 y dealingd by order of A Ds.V.S.	
"	"		S.S. Josephs surplus horses on my lines - Very inconvenient quite heavy - Health horses should have be expected to provide not white shelty.	
"	5/6/15		Lieut Saffery failed in the horse lines and for found with a great mule necessary arrangements made to remove both mental horse out it.	

"A.G." G.H.Q
    3rd Echelon
      The Base

Herewith I beg to forward copy of
War Diary to date.

                A.M Foster Capt RAVC
           O.C. 49 (W.R) Mobile Veterinary
                        Section

9/8/15.

121/6837

ans

49th Division

49th West Riding Division

Vol III

10 – 27th August 1915.

WAR DIARY
INTELLIGENCE SUMMARY.

(Erase heading not required.)

Place	Date	Hour	Summary of Events and Information	Remarks and references to Appendices
N. Poperinghe	10/8/15		H.Q. W.R.M.V.S.	
			12 Horses railed to Base today. /c Corporal Yates Pte Baker - entrained at Poperinghe - One wagon very badly ventilated - Corporal Quigley sent to S of I out to Headquarters R.A. to fetch in sick Horse. Bay Mare 40+ died en route to line - necessitated dismount of Officer. Groin with pinoline & abdomen. Wired Hopt & forwarded /is 4 R. Batteries. Horse destroyed before arrival. Case reported to A.D.V.S. for action.	
" "	12/8/15		Arranged Veterinally with owner of land 2 francs per day for hire. Report D.A.D.V.S. re water supply. Pte Hopkin 7 day lot followed by 7 day leave.	
" " " " " "	13-8-15 " "		10 Horses railed to Base /c 16. Farrier Pte Bedford, on return - Poperinghe allowed to run down into Stationary Stock without control- Some in bad Condition horses or men - Reported to A.D.V.S. Pte Say kay Brockden, on leave -	
" "	15/8/15 " "		General Parsonnel Staff inspected Lines M.V.S. Veterinary Stores arrived for the Division	

WAR DIARY or INTELLIGENCE SUMMARY

Army Form C. 2118

Place	Date	Hour	Summary of Events and Information	Remarks and references to Appendices
Steenwerck	13/8/15 14/8/15 15/8/15		Nine more horses brought from 3rd Ec. S. A. C. (W.R.) continued shoeing. Commenced to sink a well – in lines – Examined case floated from 11 Hospital Farm (4th gr. R. Cyclist Corps). Visited lines 1, 2, 3 wagon (Hy Battery) R.G.A. Much difficulty in finding exact position – Bad cases punctured wound of popliteum being furnished with Map position.	
"	14/8/15		Horse floated from 123 wagon lines – visited Cavalry Brigade at Eveningehm Shrapnel wound case – 2 pieces of shrapnel extracted – innate stock in the two wounds Neck & hindleg.	
"	15/8/15		A.D.V.S. Visited lines. General Record visited. Since subsequent expressed himself satisfied as a result.	
"	16/8/15		Sent three float to E Eveninghem c/o Corporal Yates returned with written report. Horse destroyed – 2nd Ra. the innate for Horses arrived (525.) Tried on 3 own horses	

WAR DIARY
INTELLIGENCE SUMMARY

Place	Date	Hour	Summary of Events and Information	Remarks and references to Appendices
Mzizima Camp	18/6/15		Take it quite quietly. It appears that two and might be more troops introduced up — Helmet will cover eyes as well as nose. Instruct O.R D.V.S. Yorks in information.	
" "	19/6/15		Eighteen horses railed to base from Potengah Station. Two Cases of Epizootic Lymphangitis suspected. Probable Station included. One Epizootic suspected. Plas Stockade — Cook — Clarkson. Vis Corporal in Violin. Plas Stockade — Cooke — Clarkson. Must Patrol called re well — Now reached Blue clay at 8'6" also some water. — He recommends further bore the circular. — Bore order on R.E. Stores Dept — Wiring Wedges. —	
" "	22/6/15		Visit Vet Hosp Bde Cav Horse. — Remove Shrapnel from Vendettuck floated the horse in —	
" "	23/6/15		Visit 12th, 3rd Battery of Bde R.G.A. One horse floated Dr. a. O.d. 12st Battery Horse Shot.	
" "	24/6/15		Seventeen Horses sent to base — Two Horses destroyed on lines — Recommendations for same thrown forward to Col. Macon. — Ore Case Suspected Epizootic Mange (mule) Ore Case Suspected Epizootic Mange (horse).	

WAR DIARY
or
INTELLIGENCE SUMMARY.

(Erase heading not required.)

Army Form C. 2118.

Place	Date	Hour	Summary of Events and Information	Remarks and references to Appendices
N. Potchefstroom	25/8/15		Con.D. Admitted. Carcases buried by prisoners. — P.M. Enemy made —	
	28/8/15		Float required by 2/d Battery Fd. Rly. G. — Main horses & two mules railed to Baza % Corporal Singleton. Ptes Stockdale. T. Inter- Bedford. One horse Sarcoptic Mange. One mule suspected Borbolio Mange.	
	29/6/15		No. 37 Corporal Yates detailed temporarily to act as Clerk R to A.D.V.S. Three corporals (only one N.C.O. — one of them one at the time — one permanently) into 14th Infantry Brigade. One acts as Clerk to A.D.V.S. temporarily. Recommendations for promotion have been made, & it is hoped they will be approved. — A good supply of water has been found in the well between 10 & 15 feet. Pumps wanted to make good the sides. An order to build shelters for horses has been received & S.R.V.S. asked for materials & labour.	

A.W. Foster Capt AVC

O.C. HQ VC RWT

121/7016

49th Dragoons

49 for mobile Lity. section

Sept IV
Sep 15.

WAR DIARY
or
INTELLIGENCE SUMMARY.

(Erase heading not required.)

Army Form C. 2118.

Place	Date	Hour	Summary of Events and Information	Remarks and references to Appendices
Poperinghe 2-9-15.				
	3/9/15		D.D.V.S. visited – followed boarded for Inspection Sergt. P. Greenwood. Ptes Redfern, Kelley, Stockdale, Hutton, Heveringham.	
			Twenty horses two Mules rated to trace 1/2 Corporal Single. Ptes Baker Bradley Batty. One case Sarcopt Mange included.	
	5/9/15		Veterinary stores for Division arrived by conducting party.	
	6/9/15		Three horseshoes been posted on S.M. I.T. lines the last 3 days.	
	6/9/15		Pay Parade – Rifle Inspection – Iron Ration Wallet Inspection.	
			Corporal Galoo returned to duty for duty.	
			Pte Ck. Tinker (1236) I.W.R. field ambulance admitted.	
			Pte A. Kelley R.A.M.C. proceeded on leave to England.	
			Signed agreement with owner of land. Agreement made by Lieut.	
			Stirling.	
	9/9/15		Ten horses sent to Mount Gevelainy. 3 returned. Remainder sent back.	
			N.C. cases for Mobile Veterinary Section.	
	10/9/15		J. Moon Horse. Two Mange cases Ten removing. Total 2 of Sent to trace of Bay of Bucks. Ptes Stanley. Hopkin. Redfern. Gambrell.	

WAR DIARY or INTELLIGENCE SUMMARY

Army Form C. 2118.

Place	Date	Hour	Summary of Events and Information	Remarks and references to Appendices
Mhow	9/9/15		Pte W. H. Tinker (N°12) Pte J. Butler (N°32) evacuated 87/10 C.S. invalided to England struck off strength of B. Expeditionary Force.	
	10/9/15		Appointment of N°27 Sergt H. Redfearn to 74th Infantry Brigade. N°11 Sergt A.J. Greenwood to 74th Infantry Brigade. N°21 Sergt A. Kelley to 14th & Infantry Brigade. Twenty five horses including two Mango Canoe and Set Mules evacuated to base i/c Corporal Singleton Pte Sunney Batty. Baker. Bedford.	
	13/9/15		(Sept half) Horse destroyed with Ptomaine, thereof. Fracture of Patel Bone belonging to N° Ruby Battery, No. Bde R.F.A	
	21/9/15		Ten horses (including one case of Mange) Two Mules raided to Base. Taken i/c of Gosport Yates. Private Stockton/Hinton.	
	22/9/15		General inspection of Personnel Horses Equipment, by Lieut Colonel A.W. Macent A.D.F.S. 4+9 R.D.V.Sn. - Colonel Macen allowed	

Army Form C. 2118.

WAR DIARY
or
INTELLIGENCE SUMMARY.
(Erase heading not required.)

Instructions regarding War Diaries and Intelligence Summaries are contained in F. S. Regs., Part II. and the Staff Manual respectively. Title pages will be prepared in manuscript.

Place	Date	Hour	Summary of Events and Information	Remarks and references to Appendices
	24/9/15		The men on parade - complimented them on their smartness, cleanliness & reported general satisfaction as result of his inspection. Lt. Colonel St. W. Mason O.C. V.C. proceeded on leave. Capt. & O.C. N. Foster O.C. V.C. appointed to act as O.C. V.C. No 37 Corporal C.E.N. Yates appointed to the rank of Sergeant with effect from 4-9-15. Authority 9.P.V.S. W.815 of 23-9-15.	A.N. Foster Capt. O.C. A.C.
	25/9/15		10 Horses and two Mules were Railed to Base to-day. Sergt. Baker and Pte Farror & Taylor.	A.N. Foster
	26/9/15		The need for a Float (for sick & lame horses) is very apparent. 3 Cases await the service of one now. Sometimes allowed to purchase a Float. One is very necessary for this Unit. It has not been recorded every time one has been used, but in the interests of the Service a Float should be supplied. It appears that Mobile Veterinary Sections are Sometimes	A.N. Foster Capt.
	29/9/15		12 Horses and 3 Mules Railed to the Base to-day. N/C Corporal Singleton Pte Knighton & Bradley	A.Wilk A.N. Foster
	30/9/15		Pte L.H. Stockdale proceeded to England on leave. During the month 500 Jmdn habluts for horses have been issued to Units of the Division	A.N. Foster
			Complete to 30-9-15. A.N. Foster Captain Officer Commanding Mobile Veterinary Section. 49 A.V.D.	

1577 Wt. W10791/1773 500,000 1/15 D. D. & L. A.D.S.S./Forms/C. 2118.

121/7384

49th W/Svraum

49th (WR) brotilé Vely: Lectures.

Vol V

Oct. 15

Army Form C. 2118.

WAR DIARY
or
INTELLIGENCE SUMMARY.

(Erase heading not required.)

Place	Date	Hour	Summary of Events and Information	Remarks and references to Appendices
In the Field	1-10-15		No. 66 Pte Bedford F. was admitted to 1st (W.R) Field Ambulance suffering from a kick on the fore-head.	All Rks Capt
	1-10-15		Last evening at 5 p.m. a hostile Aircraft hopped over the Lines and pieces of Shell from the Anti-aircraft Guns dropped in the Lines just clear of the Victor Lines.	A.W. Foster Capt.
	1-10-15		Corporal Singleton, Pte Knighton & Bradley returned to this Unit being on Veterinary Stores with them. This party reported by L.C. Dulling their Post Noncommissioned action taken	A.W. Foster Capt
	2-10-15		No. 55 Pte Stockdale J.H. returned from leave.	L. A.W. Foster Capt
	2-10-15		No. 18 Pte Sykes at B. appointed Barber to the Unit on 30-9-15.	O.M.
	2-10-15		Float hired to convey flour to Lines.	A.W.F
	4-10-15		Float hired to convey flour from lines to Poperinghe Station	
	4-10-15		9 Horses (1 Mangy Box included) Railed to the Base from Poperinghe Station (Sergt Yates R.E. Bailey	Foster Capt.
	4-10-15		C.Pl. 6 Private C. Bradley proceeded on leave to Eng land.	
	4-10-15		Bay Geld. belonging to the French Gendarmerie was destroyed.	
	5-10-15		No. 18 Pte Sykes A.B. admitted to 1st W.R. field amb. Peawothfall.	
	6-10-15		N. 66 Pte Bedford F. discharged to duty.	Foster Capt.

WAR DIARY
or
INTELLIGENCE SUMMARY.
(Erase heading not required.)

Army Form C.2

Place	Date	Hour	Summary of Events and Information	Remarks and references to Appendices
	5/10/15		A.D.V.S. returned from Leave.	
	6/10/15		Sergeant C.E. Hyatt, Private Cooke returned from Base. Began Veterinary Stores.	
	7/10/15		Capt. Fisher, late Veterinary Officer has been passed on leave to England.	
	15/10/15	6.30 pm	No. 18 Pte Sykes A.B. fell whilst orderly into adjusted fit - admitted to 2 Rated 1st W.R. Field Ambr. - immediately afterwards.	Seriously
	7-10-15		A.D.V.S. took Commandant Junt Vice Capt. Foster on leave.	
	9-10-15		No. 8 Pte Dunning proceeded on leave to England	
	" " "		12 Horses railed to Base from Poperinghe Station /c Pte Hunter	
	8-10-15		No. 18 Pte Sykes evacuated on to No. 4 Div. Area to No. 17 C.C.S. Fractured Fibula.	
	10/10/15		424 Dr Ryland proceeded to England on leave. No. 6 Pte Bradley C. returned from base to duty. Pte Hunter Farrier returned to this unit bringing Veterinary Stores for distribution into units of the Division.	
	11/10/15			

WAR DIARY
INTELLIGENCE SUMMARY

Army Form C. 2118.

Place	Date	Hour	Summary of Events and Information	Remarks and references to Appendices
Lulworth	13/10/15		Eleven horses railed to base from Springhead Station i/c O/Ples	
			Sgt Col. V Bedford	
	14/10/15		N° 5 Pte Winlop R.M. admitted 87th R.F. Amb. Rest Camp.	
			Capt A.N. Foster A.V.C. returned to duty from base.	
			N° 17 Pte Herringham A.V. returned to duty from base unit bringing Veterinary	
	15/10/15		Stores Indiscriminates to Divisional Units.	
			Pte Jay (or?) Bedford returned to Divisional Units.	
			N° 16 Pte Lukes A.B. evacuated to Base by F.A Ambulance	
			Train 8-10-15	
	16/10/15		15 Horses 2 Mules evacuated to Base i/c Sergeant Yates Pte	
			Stockdale, Gawlor.	
			N° 12 & 20 G.R. Gold (H.D.) taken on strong to permit	
			Horse N° 11507 Bay Geld (H.D.) evacuated 16-10-15.	
			to place 11507 Bay Geld returning to duty from base.	
			7.8 Ples Runney returned to duty from leave	
17/10/15			N° 16 Pte Sykes A.B. Attached to England Strength of the Ex Peditionary Force.	

WAR DIARY
or
INTELLIGENCE SUMMARY.
(Erase heading not required.)

Army Form C. 2118.

Place	Date	Hour	Summary of Events and Information	Remarks and references to Appendices
Sutherfield	17/10/15		N. 42 Lt. N.P. Glew reported for duty (from leave).	
	16/10/15		1/5 Pte. Winter B.M. evacuated to N/1 C.C.S.	
	18/10/15		Sergt. Yates Pte Stockdale Stanley returned to this unit bringing Veterinary Stores with them.	
			No. 30 Pte Hopkins for disrespectful language to a N.C.O was awarded forfeiture of one day's pay.	
	16/10/15		M/5 Pte Winter B.M. arms Cpl & Pavee Pte. Pte. Hopkins	
	20/10/15		Ten horses evacuated ℅ Sergt Baker	
	4 am		Horse No. 230 Roan Gelding M.D. 153rd Battery R.G.A. was destroyed "P. M. exam – revealed tuberculosis.	
	6 am		Horse No. 270 Bay Mare R.N. Mud. Battery 13. Bde R.G.A. Aged thorn was destroyed for Punctured Wound of Knee Joint (Open Hock)	
	22-10-15		Sergt. F. Baker & Pte Hopkin returned to this Unit.	A.N.T.
	25-10-15		Ten Horses & 1 Mule evacuated ℅ Sergt Yates & Pte Dunning.	A.M.T.
	26-10-15		11 Horses evacuated ℅ Pte Taylor (6 Batt).	A.N.T.
	25-10-15		Sergt. Baker & S.S. Mackey selected by the Section to be representative at a General Inspection 27/10/15	A.N.T.

WAR DIARY
or
INTELLIGENCE SUMMARY.
(Erase heading not required.)

Army Form C. 2118

Place	Date	Hour	Summary of Events and Information	Remarks and references to Appendices
In the Field	24-10-15		Application made through the A.D.V.S. 49th (W.R.) Division for a draft of 9 Privates to replace others evacuated.	A.M.F.
" "	27-10-15		Sergt Yates and Pte Jennings returned to this Unit.	A.M.F.
" "	27-10-15		Sergt Baker and S.S. Mackey represented this Unit at a General Inspection.	A.M.F.
" "	28-10-15		Private Jay Cox and Battey returned to this Unit.	
" "	29-10-15		12420 Chestnut Gld. transferred to M.V.S. Sick lines 25-10-15. Discharged to 463 Coy A.S.C. 28-10-15. 4907 Bay Gld. 7C.9 is taken on the strength of this Unit to replace 12420 Chestnut Gld. 7C.9 29-10-15.	A.M.F.
" "	30-10-15		13 Mares (Mules) evacuated to the Base to-day from Poperinghe Station. Sergt Yates, Pte Bradly.	A.M.F.
" "	30-10-15		C6-13 Pte Clarkson G. was admitted to 1 (WR) Field Ambulance this day.	A.V.F.
" "	30-10-15		Stray horse found by Sergt Rushworn A.V.C. was claimed within two hours by the King's Rifles.	A.V.F.
	31/10/15		During the current month - the Float has been required on 18 days. It has been possible to hire one.	

A. M. Foster Capt A.V.C.
O.C. 49 W.R. M.V.S.

121/7636

49th Division

49th Mach. Vet. Sec.

D Nov 1915

vol VI

Army Form C. 2118.

WAR DIARY
or
INTELLIGENCE SUMMARY.
(Erase heading not required.)

Instructions regarding War Diaries and Intelligence Summaries are contained in F. S. Regs., Part II. and the Staff Manual respectively. Title pages will be prepared in manuscript.

Place	Date	Hour	Summary of Events and Information	Remarks and references to Appendices
In the field	1-11-15		C/No 67 S.S. Mackay A.N. was granted leave from 1-11-15 to 7-11-15 to proceed to England	A.N.F.
" " "	1-11-15		Sergt Yates & Pte Bradley returned to the Unit this day.	A.N.F.
" " "	4-11-15		9 Horses & 1 Mule were Railed to the Base to-day from Poperinghe Station t/c Pte Bedford who returned	A.N.F.
" " "	3-11-15		A Party t/c Sergt F. Baker proceeded to Elverdinghe 9-30 p.m. to draw Bricks returned 9-30 p.m. (First occasion) Two Wagons	A.N.F.
" " "	4/11/15		A Party t/c Sergt F. Baker proceeded to Elverdinghe 9-30 p.m. to draw Bricks returned 2 a.m 5-11-15 (Second occasion) Two Wagons. Pte Tanner lost his N°7 Pte Goode G. detailed authorised surgical cases greatcoat.	
" " "	5/11/15		N° 23 Pte King Horace faded order. Reported t/c Sergt N. Yates Proceeded to Elverdinghe to draw bricks returned 2 a.m 6-11-15 (Third occasion) Twowagons	
" " "	6/11/15		Sergt Baker (N°15) F. was granted Leave 6-11-15 to 12-11-15. to Proceed to England —	
" "	" "		Ptes Bedford & Tanner returned to this unit to-day.	
" "	" "		A Party t/c Sergt N. Yates Proceeded to Elverdinghe to draw bricks — returned 1-30 a.m. 7 inst:—	

Army Form C. 2118.

WAR DIARY
or
INTELLIGENCE SUMMARY.
(Erase heading not required.)

Place	Date	Hour	Summary of Events and Information	Remarks and references to Appendices
In the Field	6/11/15		All units quitted their bivouacs were housed in Villots – Seventeen horses of the section were put under cover the end of last Month – Stables being constructed for the remaining seven section horses. –	
" " "	6/11/15		No 1 + 2 + 4 Dr. Glen P. A.S.C. attached to this unit was admitted to C of W.R. Field ambulance a.M. returned to duty	
" " "	" "		No 67. S.S. Waker a.M. returned to duty	
" " "	" "		Twelve Horses – 1 Mule were issued to base today ¼ of Privates Bakery & Laundry. –	
" " "	8/11/15		Nothing to report —	
" " "	" "		Veterinary Officer to HQ W.R. Div. Train (Lieut D. Kerr A.V.C.) having been granted leave Capt Foster agrees to answer for him –	
" " "	9/11/15		A. Suffolk wagon Dr (A.S.C.) 2 heavy draught horses handed to Artillery from this morning – in lieu of this wagon will stand on A.S.C. Lines.	
" " "	11-11-15		Sh 1690 Jr Wonnacott C to A.S.C. temporarily attached to this Unit to replace # 242. C.W.P.G. int. A.W. Foster	

Army Form C. 2118.

WAR DIARY
or
INTELLIGENCE SUMMARY.
(Erase heading not required.)

Instructions regarding War Diaries and Intelligence Summaries are contained in F. S. Regs., Part II. and the Staff Manual respectively. Title pages will be prepared in manuscript.

Place	Date	Hour	Summary of Events and Information	Remarks and references to Appendices
In the Field	11.11.15		A Supply Wagon & pr (A.S.C.) 2 Heavy Draught Horses are taken on the strength of this Unit from 2nd inst. to duty	A.W.F. Foster
" "	11-11-15		No 423 Pte Blackmore F. was discharged from 1/4(WR) Field Ambulance this day.	
" "	10-11-15		Ptes Baker & Fowler returned to this Unit.	
			No 5 Pte Winter B. M. invalided to England 2-11-15. Strength of officers of	A.W. Foster
			Bn. Expeditionary Force.	
			Two Wagons proceeded to Elverdinghe to draw bricks returned 12 midnight.	
" "	8-11-15		1 Wagon proceeded to Elverdinghe I/c Sergt Yates & drew bricks.	
" "	9-11-15		2 Wagons proceeded to Elverdinghe I/c Corporal Singleton to draw bricks.	
" "	10-11-15		2 Wagons proceeded to Elverdinghe I/c Sergt Yates to draw bricks.	
" "	11-11-15		2 Wagons proceeded to Elverdinghe I/c Sergt & Corpl at Sergt Yates to draw bricks.	
" "	12-11-15		2 Wagons proceeded to Elverdinghe I/c Sergt Yates. One Wagon only able to load tree owing	
" "	13-11-15		to the Village being heavily shelled.	A.W. Foster
			Order from C.R.E. not to draw Bricks from Elverdinghe until further	
" "	15-11-15		Corporal Singleton & Pte Lambert returned to this Unit.	
" "	15-11-15		15 Mens 5 Mules Railed to Bari today from Poperinghe Station I/c Sergt Baker Pte	
" "	17-11-15		Stockdale & Bedford.	

Army Form C. 2118.

WAR DIARY
or
INTELLIGENCE SUMMARY.
(Erase heading not required.)

Instructions regarding War Diaries and Intelligence Summaries are contained in F.S. Regs., Part II. and the Staff Manual respectively. Title pages will be prepared in manuscript.

Place	Date	Hour	Summary of Events and Information	Remarks and references to Appendices
In the Field	17-11-15		13099 Dvr Mara R. was evacuated to the Base to-day and is struck off the strength of this Unit.	E.W.S Foster
" "	18-11-15		A Party i/c Sergt Yates brought 2 limber loads of bricks from Elverdinghe. Sergeant Ballard, Pte Stockdale and Bedford returned to this Unit to-day.	
" "	19-11-15		2 Wagons i/c Sergt Baker proceeded to Elverdinghe to draw bricks.	
" "	20-11-15		6 Horses and 2 Mules were Railed to Base to-day from Poperinghe Station Pte Hopkins	A.W.Y Foster
" "	21-11-15		No. 424 Dvr P. Glew was discharged to duty from 1Y(WR) Field Ambulance	
" "	22-11-15		No 1690 Pte Wonnacott returned to his Unit to-day.	
" "	23-11-15		2 Wagons i/c Sergt Baker proceeded to Elverdinghe to draw bricks. Pte Hopkins J. returned to this Unit to-day.	A.W.Y Foster
" "	24-11-15		2 Wagons i/c Corporal Singleton proceeded to Elverdinghe to draw bricks	
" "	25-11-15		7 Horses 1 Mule 2 Manges Boxes including Saddlery Railed to Base to-day from Poperinghe Station i/c Sergt Baker.	
" "	27-11-15		Sergt Baker F. returned to this Unit to-day.	A.W.Y Foster
" "	27-11-15		0/149 Pte Farrand T. No 30 Pte Hardy R. having arrived as a draft from England were taken on the strength of this Unit from 26-11-15.	Capt A.W.S
" "	29-11-15		11 Horses Railed to Base to-day from Poperinghe Station i/c Corporal Singleton, Pte Houghton	

WAR DIARY
or
INTELLIGENCE SUMMARY

Army Form C. 2118.

Place	Date	Hour	Summary of Events and Information	Remarks and references to Appendices
In the Field	29-1-15		Pte. Marsh A.S.C. Transport Driver was awarded 4 days Field Punishment No 2 will solution of 4 days Pay. During the month the Fleet has been required on 6 occasions. During the month about 25 journeys have been made by 2 G.S. limbered wagons and a loading party to Elverdinghe and about 50 odds of bricks etc have been brought away for stable construction etc. Elverdinghe is about 6 mls East of these lines, and is & only frequently under Enemy Shell fire. The work of removing the bricks from semi-destroyed house is rightly and & rigid it- is fortunate that no casualties whatever have occurred owing to the bad state of the roads they wants has been severe on the Transport Horses. During the month several heavy Artillery Units which were attached to this Division for Veterinary purposes have been afford to another Veterinary Command. During the month the Railway Sidings from Hazebrouck to Poperinghe has been taken over by the British Authorities and this	A.V.K. to do Sept.

WAR DIARY
or
INTELLIGENCE SUMMARY.
(Erase heading not required.)

Army Form C. 2118.

Place	Date	Hour	Summary of Events and Information	Remarks and references to Appendices
	30-11-15		Service is improving especially with regard to shunting junctions. There are now daily in a quiet way (with consignment) to evacuate batches of sick horses. The whole of the Isolation Horse Rails and Draught are now under good hard cover and a stable to hold Patients (about twenty) is well on in construction.	

A. W. Noble?
Captⁿ A.V.C.
O.C. No 9 (W.R.) Mobile Veterinary
Section.

49th Mob. Vet. Sec".
Dare
Vol. VII

Army Form C. 2118.

WAR DIARY
or
INTELLIGENCE SUMMARY.
(Erase heading not required.)

Instructions regarding War Diaries and Intelligence Summaries are contained in F. S. Regs., Part II. and the Staff Manual respectively. Title pages will be prepared in manuscript.

Place	Date	Hour	Summary of Events and Information	Remarks and references to Appendices
In the Field	1-12-15		Corporal Singleton & Pte Knighton returned to this Unit to-day.	A.W.G Foster Capt. A.V.C
" "	3-12-15		15 Horses & 1 Mule (3 cases of Mange included) railed to the Base to-day from Poperinghe Station by Corporal Lambert Pte. Bradley & Fawley.	
" "	5-12-15		No. 31 Pte. Hardy, R. was admitted to the 1st (W.R.) Field Ambulance this day.	A.W.G Foster Capt. A.V.C
" "	6-12-15		Corporal Lambert Ptes Bradley & Fawley returned to this Unit 6-12-15	
" "	6-12-15		9 Horses and 2 Mules Railed to Base to-day from Poperinghe Station by Sergt Baker and Pte Bedford.	
" "	6-12-15		No. 37 Sergt. Yates G.E.M. was granted leave to England 6-12-15 to 13-12-15	A.W.G Foster Captain A.V.C
" "	8-12-15		Sergt. Baker & Pte Bedford returned to this Unit to-day.	
" "	9-12-15		15 Horses 1 Remount Car included railed to Base to-day from Poperinghe Station by Corporal Singleton & Pte Farrer.	
" "	8-12-15		Light Draught Horses & Mules ordered to be handed over from 49th to 14th Division (Under orders to proceed to Egypt), have to be tested with Mallein by the Officer i/c the Town Major of Poperinghe. Letter of instruction from O. S.M.V.S. were delivered to executive Veterinary Officers of this Division by Orderlies from the M.V.S. There was delay.	A.W.G Foster Capt. A.V.C

WAR DIARY
or
INTELLIGENCE SUMMARY.
(Erase heading not required.)

Army Form C. 2118.

Place	Date	Hour	Summary of Events and Information	Remarks and references to Appendices
In the Field	8-12-15		On the arrival of the Mallein from Hazebrouck. It was to arrive at 12 noon but arrived at 5-30 p.m. and was delivered to V.O.s i/c Units immediately.	A.M. Tosh Capt.
" "	10-12-15		No 31 Pte Hardy R. was discharged to duty from 1st (W.R.) Field Ambulance this day.	
" "	10-12-15		No 312 Dr. Cahill J. A.S.C. was granted leave to proceed to England from 11-12-15 to 16-12-15.	AM.
" "	11-12-15		Corporal Singleton Pte. Farror returned to this Unit to-day.	V.T.C
" "	11-12-15		No 22 Pte Hinton W.H. was admitted to 1/1st (W.R.) Field Ambulance this day.	Loss
" "	12-12-15		15 Horses (9 Remount cases included) evaced to Base to-day from Poperinghe Station	day A.M.O.
" "			1/c Corporal Lambert - Pte Cooke, Starkey.	
" "	12-12-15		C.C.M.V.S. arrived V.O. 1/c 4/9 (W.R.) Div. A.C. to Mallein Animals to be handed over to 14 bump in that Unit.	AM.
" "			No 22 Pte Linton N.H. A.V.C. 4/9(W.R) M.V.S. was evacuated to No 12 C.C.S Sunday.	
" "	13-12-15		C.C.M.V/S inspected 30 Horses at the lines of the 4/9 (W.R) D.A.C. (Mallein Test). No Reactors.	AM.
" "	13-12-15		C.C.M.V/S distributed 138 Horses at the lines of 463 Bty A.S.C 49 (W.R) Division.	AM.
" "	14-12-15		11 Horses 1 Mule (Shrant cases included) Railed to Base to-day from P'ghue Stn. I/c Corporal Singleton & Pte Knighton.	AM. Tosh captain

WAR DIARY
or
INTELLIGENCE SUMMARY.

Army Form C. 2118.

Place	Date	Hour	Summary of Events and Information	Remarks and references to Appendices
In the Field	4-12-15		Corporal Lambert, Pte Cogher & Hardy returned to the Unit to-day.	A M Foster Capt
" "	16-12-15		Horse & Mule raid to the Base to-day from Poperinghe Station 1/c Pte Taylor 7.P.P.	
" "	16-12-15		C.E. M.V.S. visited the lines of the H(W.R.)D. O.C.E. & 1st (W.R.)B. O.C.E. and Inoculated Mules with Mallein.	A M Foster Capt
" "	18-12-15		No. 9 Pte Forrand. E was admitted to 1st (W.R.) Field Ambulance.	
" "	20-12-15		No. 9 Pte Forrand. E. was evacuated to No. 17 C.C.S.	
" "	21-12-15		The following N.C.O. and men were granted leave to England from 21-12-15 to 28-12-15. No. 115 Corporal Lambert. G. A.V.C. No. 43. Pte Clarkson G. A.V.C. 66 Pte Bedford F A.V.C. 69 Pte Baker R A.V.C. 53 Pte Fawley A.V.C. 7 Pte Cooke G A.V.C.	A M F Capt
" "	19-12-15		C.E. M.V.S. took Veterinary Charge of the following Units. 1st (W.R.)B. R.F.E. 146th Inf. Bde. 2nd (W.R.) Field Ambulance.	
" "	23/12/15		A.V.S. Poperinghe leave Capt Foster G.F. A.D.V.S.	
" "	25-12-15		Horse raid to the Base to-day from Poperinghe Station 1/c Sergt Yates (W Harrow) Corporal Singleton to Pte Dunning returned to this Unit to-day.	
" "	26-12-15		C.E. M.V.S. went to Boys in men to Reve fuppy & Haynage and collected Hay from M. Salier Vaz denberghe which had been lighting him 9-10-15 by 24 D.O.E.	A M Foster Capt

WAR DIARY
or
INTELLIGENCE SUMMARY.
(Erase heading not required.)

Army Form C. 2118.

Place	Date	Hour	Summary of Events and Information	Remarks and references to Appendices
In the Field	27.9.15		Sergt. Jacobs R.F. over returned to this Unit to-day.	O.M.S
" "	27.9.15		Monsieur Gillam, Belgian Interpreter is taken on the strength of this Unit from 26th Sept.	
" "	28.9.15		28 Horses & Mules railed to the Base to-day from Popringhe Station i/c Mount Singleton Pte Bradley Dunning & Hardy.	Pte Bradley
" "	28.9.15		A.D.V.S. inspected 148 Infantry Bde.	
" "	28.9.15		Visited lines of 3rd Batt. 1st W.R.B. R.F.A. destroyed Bay mare.	O.M.S
" "	28.9.15		A.D.V.S. Pulventerhinter N.K. Osthoj Comb.	Pte Jack Coyff.
" "	28.9.15		Visited Div: Train lines for distribution of horses to 2 Rem. Horses did not arrive - arranged distribution to-morrow.	
" "		2 p.m		
" "	30.9.15		38 Horses & Mules Rd.d. to the Base to-day from Popringhe Station i/c B/M ambulance Pte Fawley Farrier Cooper King & Pte.	O.M.S
" "	29.9.15		S/Sgt Baker, brother Blacksmiths Fowler returned to this Unit to-day.	Pte Cooper.
" "	30.9.15		No. 56 Pte Boyd milk R. returned to this Unit to-day.	
" "	30.9.15		M.V.S. visited 1/3 Field Amb. and conveyed Blech 601 (Mare) suffering.	

1577 Wt.W10791/1773 500,000 1/15 D.D.&L. A.D.S.S./Forms/C. 2118.

WAR DIARY
INTELLIGENCE SUMMARY

Army Form C. 2118.

Place	Date	Hour	Summary of Events and Information	Remarks and references to Appendices
Camp in the field	30/12/15		Horse Pan - Contents of the N.H. ech. Bay held very emaciated suffering	A.M. Foster
			from Pneumonia. Hopeless case. Both animals telegraphed in't to R.J. Betat Capt.	
			Notification by Telegram sent to the G.O.C. 167 Infantry Brigade.	
			Capt P.P. Sutland R.A.V.C. reported to D.D.V.S. 8.30 pm for temporary	
R.l. field 29-12-15			duty with 49th (W.R.) Divison. Posted to 1st (W.R.) Brigade R.T.o. 30-12-15	

A.M. Foster
Capt RAVC Mobile Veterinary
(W.R.) Section
c/o 49 (W.R.) Division

31-12-15

MOBILE VETERINARY SECTION
31-12-15
49th (W.R.) DIVISION

Agr. D. Mrs. Vac. Sec.

Jan 1916

Vol VIII

WAR DIARY
or
INTELLIGENCE SUMMARY.

Army Form C. 2118.

Place	Date	Hour	Summary of Events and Information	Remarks and references to Appendices
In the Field	1-1-16		22 Horses were railed to the Base from Pepenghe Station i/c Pte Stockdale, Bed and Hardy.	A.M. & Foster
Ledringhem	3-1-16 2-1-16		Pte Stockdale, Bedford & Hardy returned to this Unit 1/5 day. M.V.S. handed over Camp & Stores at N's 12, C 3, 10 to N. D.V. Cyclist Section proceeded to new Area N taking hay - C 29, a 6.4. - Clarence Mo[bile] School 29. Marched through Proven - Chat. at Hondzame - 1½ hrs. halt to transport become up and to consume rations & water & feed horses - Old lines left at 10. a.m. New lines reached 7.4-15 p.m. Rain commenced 12 noon - halt & tents were blown down - Through Mergele, Wormhoult - Good roads all the way - Good billets at Oudhaves Farm - Cover for horses & men.	A.M.&. Foster Capt
In the Field	7-1-16		No 22 Pte Linton W.H. was discharged from the Convalescent Camp 1-1-16 and was detailed at No 3 Veterinary Hospital to rejoin this Unit and reported for duty 7-1-16.	A.M.& Foster
"	7-1-16		No 9 Pte Farrand. E. invalided to England 30/12-15 and is struck off the strength of the Expeditionary Force accordingly.	E.V.F.

Army Form C. 2118.

WAR DIARY
or
INTELLIGENCE SUMMARY.
(Erase heading not required.)

Instructions regarding War Diaries and Intelligence Summaries are contained in F. S. Regs., Part II. and the Staff Manual respectively. Title pages will be prepared in manuscript.

Place	Date	Hour	Summary of Events and Information	Remarks and references to Appendices
In the field	8-1-16		29 Horses & 3 Mules were railed to the Base to-day from Armake Station. Lt Sergt Yates Pte Bradley Baker & Cooke.	3 All tack Capt
" "	8-1-16		O.C. M.V.S. finished the fixing of (No 2 (W.R.)) 7 Coy R.E. report to A.D.V.S. vide Letter Book No 478.	All tack Capt W.R.
" "	8-1-16		O.C. M.V.S. visited the lines of 7 Coy 1st Labour Battⁿ R.E. report to A.D.V.S. vide Letter Book No 477.	Capt W.R.
" "	8-1-16		No 67 S.S. A/t Mahan appointed Barber to this Unit will pay at 6ᵈ p.d. to be paid out of Canteen accounts.	A.N. tack Capt W.R.
" "			Capts. 6 Corpl A 1066 dated 4-1-16. Captain A.M. Foster A.V.C proceeded on leave to England 10-1-16 to 17-1-16	Capt W.R.
" "	10-1-16		No 4 Pte Stockton J.G. proceeded on leave to England 10-1-16 to 17-1-16	A.M.F.
" "	10-1-16		No 53 Pte Taylor J. was this day awarded 3 extra guards for absence from Camp (No conf in removal of a horse).	A.W. Foot Sergt
" "	10-1-16		Lieut Colonel A.W. Mason A.V.C took over the command of this Unit	Capt W.R.
" "	11-1-16		36 Horses and 1 Mule (1 case of Mange included) were railed to the Base to day from Armake Station. The l/Cpl Pt & orderly Ptes C Larkeron & Hardy.	A.V.C

WAR DIARY
or
INTELLIGENCE SUMMARY.
(Erase heading not required.)

Army Form C. 2118.

Place	Date	Hour	Summary of Events and Information	Remarks and references to Appendices
No.16 Mobile Vety	11-1-16		Sergt Yates Pte Bolan, Bradley, Cooke returned to this Unit 11-1-16	
" "	12-1-16		No 185 (Bay Gyd) HD 4163 Coy ASC attached to this Unit for supplies died on Afnoon of 11 inst. A Post-mortem examination was made by Lieut Muir AVC which revealed a Tumr of the Large Bowel.	
" "	13-1-16		16 Horse were railed to the Base 13-day from Armche Station (Sergt Yates Pte Knight)	
" "	14-1-16		Corporal Lambert Pte Hardy & Clarkson returned to this Unit.	
" "	15-1-16		23 Horse & 1 Mule (2 cases of Mange included) were railed to the Base to-day from Armche Station. Sergt Chfy Lambert Pte Jinton & Hardy	
" "	16-1-16		Sergt Yates & Pte Knighton returned to this Unit 16-day.	
" "	18-1-16		Corporal Lambert, Pte Jinton & Fawley returned to this Unit to-day.	
" "	20-1-16		15 Horse 2 Mule (4 cases of Mange included) were railed to the Base to-day from Armche Station Yc Sergt Wates Pte Taylor & Stordale.	
" "	21-1-16		Captain C.M. Foster AVC resumed command of this Unit.	
" "	21-1-16		No 4 Pte Stockton L.C. Gye returned to this Unit to-day.	
" "	22-1-16		In accordance with Army Council Instructions No 16 of Jan 1916 dated H.O. 5-1-16 the following will be the designation of the No 16 Mobile Veterinary Section	

W.S. Foster
Capt
AVC

WAR DIARY or INTELLIGENCE SUMMARY

Army Form C. 2118.

Place	Date	Hour	Summary of Events and Information	Remarks and references to Appendices
In the Field	22-1-16		of the H.Q.(H.R.)Division 1/1st (H.R.) Mobile Veterinary Section.	
" "	24-1-16		No. 39 Pte Hopkin F. ANC was granted leave to England from 23-1-16 to 30-1-16	A.W. Foster Capt
" "	24-1-16		14 Horses & 1 Mule (4 cases of Mange included) were railed to the Base to-day from Crouha Station 1/c Sergt Barker, Pte Knighton & Dunning.	
" "	25-1-16		26 Section Horses 2 attached were tested with Mallein (intra-dermal) and passed the test.	
" "	25-1-16		C.2. Bay Mule Gld was destroyed. A Post-Mortem Examination was made of the Animal by the O/C. M.V.S. which revealed a Comminuted Fracture of the 1/ N. Femur.	
" "	26-1-16		Sergt Barker, Pte Knighton & Dunning returned to this Unit to-day	A.W. Foster Capt A.V.C
" "	27-1-16		19 Horses 2 Mules (1 case of Mange & 2 Ringworm included were railed to the Base to-day from Angres Station i/c Corporal Lambert & Pte Knighton.	
" "	30-1-16		Corporal Lambert & Pte Knighton returned to this Unit to-day	
" "	30-1-16		No 68 Pte Taylor T.J.S. is appointed (unpaid) Lance-Corporal from Jan 30th 1916	A.W. Foster Capt
" "	30-1-16		No 295 Bay Mare H D was destroyed. Double Gangrenous Pneumonia (Chronic age and emaciation. P/Mortem Exam showed also complete rupture of oesophagus.	

WAR DIARY
or
INTELLIGENCE SUMMARY.

(Erase heading not required.)

Place	Date	Hour	Summary of Events and Information	Remarks and references to Appendices
In the field	31-1-16		35 Horses (3 Mules (4 cases of Mange included) were railed to the Base to-day from Armahe Station. L/Sergt Bolan Pte Bradley, Junior, Bedford, Fawley & Hardy.	
" " "	31-1-16		No 39 Pte Hopkin J. W.C. returned to this Unit to-day.	
" " "	28-1-16		D.D.V.S. 2nd Army visited and inspected the Section afterwards paraded the Officer, N.C.O's and Men, complimented them on the work they had done the good discipline shown, and wished them good-bye and good luck.	
" " "	31-1-16		Orders to be ready to move 1 at short notice have been received and also sealed orders to be opened at destination.	

A. N. Foster
Capt" A.V.C.

C.O. 11th (W.R.) M.V.S.

[Stamp: MOBILE VETERINARY SECTION No. Date 31-1-16 49th (W.R.) DIVISION]

49

1/1 W.R. Mob Vety Sec
Vol. IX

WAR DIARY
or
INTELLIGENCE SUMMARY.
(Erase heading not required.)

Army Form C. 2118.

Place	Date	Hour	Summary of Events and Information	Remarks and references to Appendices
In the Field	2-2-16		Sergt Bahn, Ptes Bradley, Fawley, Linton, Hardy & Bedford returned to this Unit to-day.	
" "	2-2-16		18 O.Rs (including 2 Corps of Mange & 2 officers were railed to the Base to-day from Gonnehem Station "Lillers" & L'Enforcé Gambut.	
" "	3-2-16		The Section vacated Billets at Lidinghem and marched to Bavinchove. Departed Station in Bavinchove (March 2 hours) entrained there. (Time taken to entrain 20 minutes). After several hours train journey during which there was no opportunity to water & feed horses Long night was spent at Ful Station 2 am 4. Horses reached and orders received to detrain. Time of detrainment 12-39 am. 4 February (Lynn 1hr 20 minutes) Such time collected. Upon entraining	
" "	4-2-16	1 pm	Marched through Cunsiès. Halted by River side watered & fed horses & rationed men.	
" "	" "	2 pm	Marched off — Proceeded through Hoget Anyens — Druril – Arsilly — and on to Picquigny where a halt of three-quarters of an hour was made. Horses watered & fed. and our Billets located. March continued to Belloy-sur-Somme where the Section took over the Billets vacated by	

Army Form C. 2118.

WAR DIARY
or
INTELLIGENCE SUMMARY.

(Erase heading not required.)

Place	Date	Hour	Summary of Events and Information	Remarks and references to Appendices
H. Hill	4-2-16		"Mobile Veterinary Corporal Lambert Justin & Duprieux returned to this Unit to-day.	
" "	5-2-16		Nos 25, 4 & 9,650 Pte Durand W.S. attained H. Platts w/H Art. arrived as a draft from England and are taken on the strength of this Unit from 5-2-16.	
" "	10-2-16		21 Horses 1 Mule (6 cases of Mange included) Railed to Rouen to-day from Hangest Station. i/c Coun - Corporal Taylor, Pte Bedford Storkdale & Hadley.	
" "	10-2-16		No 10 Pte Farrer A.W. granted leave to England from 12-2-16 to 19-2-16.	
" "	13-2-16		7 Horses were Railed to Rouen to-day from Hangest Station i/c Corporal Lambert. The Section vacated Billets at Belloy to-day to New-Area Sergt Yates and 1 Private were left i/c of charge of Billets & 4 sick horse to hand over to In-coming M.V.S. The march was commenced 5-30 a.m. and the route taken was that through La Chaussée, St Sauveur, Breilly, Bertangles, Coisy, Raimville. From to Mossligny-au-Bois to this an hours halt was made, horse watered f/s and the men consumed rations carried. 1 km Molliens was left and the Section proceeded through Beaucourt, S Contay to Vadencourt reaching	

WAR DIARY
or
INTELLIGENCE SUMMARY.
(Erase heading not required.)

Army Form C. 2118.

Place	Date	Hour	Summary of Events and Information	Remarks and references to Appendices
In the Field	14-2-16		there 3-30 p.m. where New billets were taken up.	
" "	15-2-16		3 Sick horses taken over from No 42 M.V.S. in Contay	
" "	23-2-16		19 horses 1 Mule (6 cases of Mange included) railed to Pargny-to-day from Méricourt Station. Yeomen Depl. Taylor, Pte Hunningham & Baker	
" "	22-2-16		Corporal A. Smyglon A.V.C. granted leave to Eng Cand 22-2-16 to 29-2-16	
" "	20-2-16		No 45 Corporal L. Lambert A.V.C. temporarily attached 148 Bry Bde.	
" "			Actd. far Sergt. Kelley A.C. Cpl granted leave 20-2-16	
" "	24-2-16		Captain Porton. anowering for Captn Lewis on leave 24-2-16	
" "	23-2-16		Captain a.w. Foster received Remounts at Méricourt 10-30 p.m 86 Mules, 134 b	
			22 L.D.	
" "	24-2-16		Captain a.w. Forste distributed Remounts 10 am Don Train Lines.	
" "	29-2-16		15 horses (7 cases of Mange included) railed to Base to-day from Méricourt Station. 1/c Sergt Bakewell Pte Bradley	

29-2-16

a.w. Foster.
Capt. A.V.C.
O.C. V.S. (MR) MRS.

49

1/1 W.R. [illegible] Vely Lee
Vol X

WAR DIARY
or
INTELLIGENCE SUMMARY
(Erase heading not required.)

Army Form C. 2118.

Place	Date	Hour	Summary of Events and Information	Remarks and references to Appendices
In the field	2-3-16		2 Horses & 4 Mules (1 case of Mange included) railed to Bar to-day from Mericourt Station i/c Corporal Lambert. Pte Atkinson, Cooke, Dunning & Fawley.	A.W. Fage Capt. A.V.C.
" "	4-3-16		10 Horses & 1 Mule railed to Bar to-day from Mericourt Station i/c Corporal Singleton & Pte Farrer. Cpl Lambert, Pte Atkinson, Cooke, Dunning & Fawley returned this Unit.	
" "	5-3-16		Boarded & floated from No 42 MVS and floated a horse from Heplainville to No 3B MVS at Retirmont (informing the O/C of that Unit. Corporal Singleton & Pte Farrer returned to this Unit. The Horse floated to No-30 MVS was transferred to No-12 MVS.	
" "	6-3-16		Captain C.M. Foster relinquished temporary charge of Divisional Troops and Captain J. Kerr resumed duty.	
" "	4-3-16		Captain Wood A.V.C. consulted 6 p.m. 2 o'clock a.m. with reference to mule illness amongst mules of 148th Infantry Brigade Machine Gun Section at Harley. The illness commenced the night of 4-3-16. 4 have been attacked & died within 18 hours of onset of symptoms. Carcases had been buried. Post-Mortem examination of Mule remaining sicken showed	

Place	Date	Hour	Summary of Events and Information	Remarks and references to Appendices
In the Field	5-3-16		Stomach full of ungrated laugh compound of crushed Maize contents. At times very fluid particles of Maize adhering to Bowel walls. Liver & Kidneys pale very soft, easily broken down.	
" "	6-3-16		The two living water Animals whose condition was noted to have improved with chill not properly conscious of food, bowels in-active Pylon very full, temperature fluctuating before rectal temperature fluctuating. There was marked swelling over part of leg, the typical mucous membrane was ulcerated & sluffing and there was a slight blood-stain watery discharge from the nostril. It was considered that the condition arose from the poisonous action of something in general. A Dose of Arecoline (intra-muscular) was administered to each and faeces very black and granular-coated were voided. The Animals rapidly lost flesh but in other respects their condition improved slightly and were taken over by Mobile Veterinary Section on the afternoon of the 6th inst.	

WAR DIARY or INTELLIGENCE SUMMARY

Army Form C. 2118.

Place	Date	Hour	Summary of Events and Information	Remarks and references to Appendices
In the Field	6-3-16		Under orders from Divn. Headquarters the Section vacated its Billets at Vadencourt and took up new ones at Beaucourt.	
" "	10-3-16		Move commenced at 8-30 pm and finished at 10-30 am. 14 Horses (4 cases of Mange included) railed to Base to-day from Mericourt Station.	
" "	10-3-16		L/c Sergt. Yates. Pte Hardy & Hopkins. Detachment N.5 (WB) Field Coy R.E. being duty at Saw Mill Beaucourt attached to 1/1 (WB) M.V.S. for rations. Further orders notice.	
" "	8-3-16		Captain J. Baker provided to No. 5 Veterinary Hospital Abbeville i/c of a E.S. Limbered Wagon to exchange for a Cart.	
" "	12-3-16		Sergt. Yates Pte Hardy & Hopkins returned to this Unit to-day Baths having been allotted at Beauchencourt the Section was paraded there this morning and the Baths appear to be popular.	
" "	12-3-16			
" "	13-3-16		Two Horses belonging to the 2/2nd Highland Field Coy R.E. collected from a Civilian inhabitant of Mollens-au-Bois.	
" "	15-3-16		27 Horses (cases of Mange included) railed to Base to-day from Mericourt Station.	

WAR DIARY or INTELLIGENCE SUMMARY

Army Form C. 2118.

Place	Date	Hour	Summary of Events and Information	Remarks and references to Appendices
In the Field	15.3.16		No 17 Pte Heveningham A.S. admitted 1/3rd (WR) Field Ambulance	
" "	16.3.16		No 49 Pte Atkinson H. admitted 1/3rd (WR) Field Ambulance	
" "	17.3.16		No 424 Dr. P.G. Luv admitted 1/3rd (WR) Field Ambulance	
" "	19.3.16		No 17 Pte Heveningham A.S. discharged from Hospital	
" "	20.3.16		Bar Gold H.D. attacked with Violent Colic 6.30 pm died before 8 pm. P.M. examination of Bay Gold "B" also attacked at same time. Black Gold "B w.h. Anthrax" Smears sent to London report to ADVS 21.3.16	
" "	20.3.16		Sergt E.E.A. Hyde sent as relief for ADVS Clerk.	
" "	21.3.16		No 49 Pte Atkinson H. discharged from Hospital	
" "	21.3.16		Horse 1 Mule collected from Evacuees	
" "	23.3.16		Dr. Booker temporarily attached to replace Dr.G.Luv while in Hospital.	
" "	23.3.16		Dr. G. Luv discharged from Hospital	
" "	23.3.16		8 Horses railed to Boen to-day from Miraucourt Station ℅ Lieut Taylor.	
" "	23.3.16		Section Hagee included in the open under Divisional Orders	
" "	25.3.16		Orders having been received 7 pm 24th inst. to evacuate Beaumont the Unit marched out of that village and took up Billets at Mailley au Bois. March of 9.30 am arrived 11 am. All horses picketed in the open	

WAR DIARY
or
INTELLIGENCE SUMMARY.

(Erase heading not required.)

Army Form C. 2118.

Place	Date	Hour	Summary of Events and Information	Remarks and references to Appendices
In the Field	27.3.16		14 Horses / Mule (2 cases of Mange included) railed to Base to-day from Corbie Station. i/c Sergt Baker & Pte Pratt.	
" "	28.3.16		8 Horses (2 cases of Mange included) railed to Base to-day from Corbie Station. i/c Corporal Hamblet.	
" "	29.3.16		No 8 Pte J. Dunning admitted 2nd (W.R.) Field Ambulance.	
" "	29.3.16		Sergt F. Baker & Pte Pratt returned to this Unit.	
" "	29.3.16		Unit vacated Billets at Mollens au Bois. Marched off 2.30pm via Villers-Bocage - Flesselles - Havernas - to Canaples where Billets were taken up 7pm.	
" "	29.3.16		Sick Horse was left at Mollins-au-Bois i/c of Private Stockdale.	
" "	31.3.16		Major-General Perceval Commanding 49 (W.R.) Division inspected the Lines to-day at 11.25pm.	
" "	31.3.16		Horse belonging to the 4th (W.R.) Howitzer Bde R.F.A. collected from an Lieu inhabited at Harponville - Floated in.	

A.U. Foster
Capt.in
 R.A.V.C. (W.R) M.V.S
C.C. 1/1 (W.R.)

[Stamp: MOBILE VETERINARY SECTION * 49th (W.R.) DIVISION * No. Date 31-3-16]

A.D.S.S./Forms/C. 2118.

49

Mob Vely Sect

Vol XI

WAR DIARY
or
INTELLIGENCE SUMMARY.
(Erase heading not required.)

Army Form C. 2118.

Place	Date	Hour	Summary of Events and Information	Remarks and references to Appendices
In the Field	3-4-16		Captain Foster member of board of Officers, President Major Walker, 6th (W.R.) Regt. Lieut. Cuthill other member at Naours to examine Sergt. Milner 4th W.R. Regt. Subject- Shoeing — Finding Practical & reliable shoeing-smith.	
" "	4-4-16		18 Horse & 3 Mule (1 one of many included) raid to Bray to-day from Candas Station. N/c Sergt Yates Pte Hardy & Drvr Blew	
" "	5-4-16		Nos 5 & 6 Pte J. Dunning & C. Bradley discharged to duty from 3 (W.R) Field Ambulance.	
" "	6-4-16		Capt. A. M. Porter acting A.D.V.S. for Col: Moore on leave.	
" "	7-4-16		19 Horse raid to Bapa to-day from Candas Station N/c Cpl Singleton Pte Baker & Cook.	
" "	9-4-16		Cpl Singleton Pte Baker & Cook returned to this Unit to-day.	
" "	10-4-16		46 horse raid to Bryon to-day from Candas Station N/c Corporal Lambert Pte Stocksdale, A. Pinkney, Pratt, Hughes & Bradley.	
" "	11-4-16		No 8 Pte T. Dunning admitted 4th (WR) Field Ambulance.	
" "	13-4-16		20 Horse 1 Mule raid to Bray to-day from Candas Station N/c Sergt Baker Pte Foster, Bradford & Bradley.	

WAR DIARY
or
INTELLIGENCE SUMMARY.
(Erase heading not required.)

Army Form C. 2118.

Place	Date	Hour	Summary of Events and Information	Remarks and references to Appendices
In the Field	13-4-16		Pte Linton G Batty returned to this Unit from Depot. Have in England (5-4-16 to 12-4-16)	
"	14-4-16		Sergt - F Bahn, Pte Bufford, Farrar, & Pte Bradley returned to this Unit.	
"	14-4-16		Nos 58 - Pte E.H. Stothdale relected for appointment as Regimental Transport Officer. Entrained at Conghea Station at 5-8 pm this unit. To Report to D.A.Q.	
"			Have Been on arrival trip.	
"	14-4-16		No 8 Pte J. Dinning discharged to duty from 1/1 (W.R) Field Ambulance	
"	17-4-16		16 Horse & Mules (5 Bens & Mange inclided) moved to Bon to day from bombes	
"			Station 1/c Janues & Pte Taylor Pte Pikernon & Darrand	
"			Lieut-Colonel A W Mason returned from leave, Captain A.N. Foster reared	
"	19-4-16		is out as A.D.V.S.	
"	1-4-16		Horse collected from Naours 170" Bde R.F.A.	
"	8-4-16		2 Horse collected from Beauval 89" Field Ambulance	
"	11-4-16		2 Horses collected from Villers-nons-Ailly 147 Bde R.F.A. 2.9" Division	
"	12-4-16		1 Horse collected from Villers-nons-Ailly 18" London Regiment	
"	13-4-16		9 Mule collected from Domart-en-Ponthieu	
"	17-4-16		Visited Domart interview with Major, no British animals in his charge report to A.D.V.S. 49" (N.R) Division	

WAR DIARY or INTELLIGENCE SUMMARY

Army Form C. 2118.

Place	Date	Hour	Summary of Events and Information	Remarks and references to Appendices
In Field	14-4-16		Horse collected from Candas. 1/1st London Bde R.F.A.	
" "	15-4-16		Manger Tombrichan from 6th Valheureux reported direct to D.D.V.S. & Army	
" "	15-4-16		2 Horse Trench-Mortar School in field and admd upon reports dutto	
" "	16-4-16		Horse collected from 1st Auxiliary Horse Transport Company Bois de Fleurie.	
" "	19-4-16		35 Animals received from Divisional Unit East Eng D.D.R. & Army	
" "	20-4-16		40 Horse 3 Mules railed to Boves 15-day from Candas Station 1/c Sgt Yates Pte Bradley, Bedford, Baker, Knighton Pratt Hardy	
" "	20-4-16		No. 20 Pte E. Bath A.V.C. admitted 1/(1st) Field Ambulance	
" "	24-4-16		No. 20 Pte E. G. Bath A.V.C. Discharged to duty from 1/(H.P.) Field Ambulance	
" "	25-4-16		D.D.V.S. toured Horse vehicles and inspected horse-shoe unit Sgt. Baker, Sgt Yates examined Chiddington, Lambert, L/Cpl Taylor, Pte S. Mackey, Pte Baker, Hopkin Linton, Heveningham, Cooke, Bedford.	
" "	26-4-16		Captain J.R. Foster received Paratyphoid inoculation	
" "	27-4-16		11 Horses (2 cases of mange included) railed to Rawkesby from Candas Station.	
" "	28-4-16		1/c Cpl Lambert, Pte Jam Pte Denning. Sgt Baker, Pte Baker, Bedford, Bradley, Atkinson, De Cahill received Paratyphoid inoculation	

WAR DIARY or INTELLIGENCE SUMMARY

Army Form C. 2118.

Place	Date	Hour	Summary of Events and Information	Remarks and references to Appendices
Ch. McIntyres	29-4-16		Cpl Lambert, Pte Dunning returned from Base. No 4.3 Pte G.J. Blackson awarded 3 days Field Punishment No 1 – with loss of 3 day's pay. Disobeying Standing Order. During the month Horse No 13090 Chest. Gelda 18.15.2 agm. Mar. Ipol f.f.f. set N.H. fetlock evacuated to Base for debility. C.2 Black Mare R. 15h. 7yrs Col. Saddle 1.H. heel. Taken on Strength to replace above. No. 36 Black Mare H.D. 16.2. 6 yrs Mar. unobthp B.F. leg taken on strength to replace Bay Gelds. H.D. which died that month.	

A. M. Foster
Capt. F.V.C.
O.C. 4 (W.R.) M.V.S.

WAR DIARY
or
INTELLIGENCE SUMMARY.
(Erase heading not required.)

Army Form C. 2118.

1/1 WR Mob Vet Sec
Vol 12

Place	Date	Hour	Summary of Events and Information	Remarks and references to Appendices
In the Field	1-5-16		9 Horses (1 case of Vice included) railed to Base today from Candas Station	A.M.L.
"	1-5-16		To Corporal A. Singleton, Sergts Yates, Pte Barrand, Cooke, Queeny, Farrar, & Hurley received Paratyphoid inoculation.	
"	3-5-16		Corporal Singleton, Ptes Venton, Hersey, Brighton, Batt. D. Pte Henry Paratyphoid inoculation.	
"	4-6-16		9 Horses railed to Base today from Candas Station. To Sergt Baker and Pte Farrar.	
"	6-5-16		No. 50. Pte. M.B. Pratt. A.V.C. Proceeded to No 22 Veterinary Hospital, Abbeville, to undergo a course of instruction in farriery.	
"	8-5-16		No. 68 Lance Cpl (A/C) F.J.S. Taylor AVC granted leave to England from 9-5-16 to 16-5-16	
"	9-5-16		Captain A.M. Forster AVC visited the lines of the 46th Reserve Park ASC at Fienvillers and inspected 110 Remounts	
"	11-5-16		6 Horses 2 Mules (1 case of Mange included) railed to Base today from Candas Station i/c Sergt Yates.	

Army Form C. 2118.

WAR DIARY
or
INTELLIGENCE SUMMARY.
(Erase heading not required.)

Instructions regarding War Diaries and Intelligence Summaries are contained in F. S. Regs., Part II. and the Staff Manual respectively. Title pages will be prepared in manuscript.

Place	Date	Hour	Summary of Events and Information	Remarks and references to Appendices
In the Field	15-3-16		22 Horses 1 Mule railed to Base to-day from Candas Station i/c L/Cpl Lambert Pte Bedford & Baker	
" "	16-3-16		6 Horses 2 Mules railed to Base to-day from Candas Station i/c Cpl Swigton & Pte Darrand. 1 Horse (Punct Wound N. Haunch) died en Route.	C.A.V.C.
" "	18-3-16		L/Cpl Swigton & Pte Darrand returned to this Unit	
" "	17-3-16 6pm		Captain A.N. Fortin AVC proceeded on leave to England	
" "			Granted leave from 19-5-16 to 29-3-16	
" "	17-3-16		Captain D. Klein VAVC acting O.C. 1/:("uk) MVS	
" "	18-3-16		No 37 Sergt. E.B. H Yates AVC proceeded on leave to England 19-3-16 to 26-3-16	
" "	18-5-16		No 424 Dvr P.G. Glew A.S.C proceeded on leave to England 19-5-16 to 26-3-16	
" "	18-5-16		No 68 Pte (L/Cpl) F.G.S. Taylor AVC returned to this Unit from 7 days in England.	
" "	22-3-16		4 Horses 2 Mules railed to Base to-day from Candas from Candas Station i/c Lance Cpl Taylor Ptes Pawley & Sinton (1 Mare with foal at foot included)	

T.P. 81. W⁺. W708-776. 500000. 4/16. Sir J.C. & S.

Place	Date	Hour	Summary of Events and Information	Remarks and references to Appendices
In the Field	22-5-16		Lieut-Colonel Maron AVC. (a.D.V.S. 49th (WR) Division) arrived & is of. to take over the 1st (WR) M.V.S.	
" "	25-5-16		10 horses 1 mule railed to Base to-day from Candas Station	
			No 37 Sergt C.E. Yate AVC returned to this Unit from 7 days leave in England	
" "	27-5-16		No 424 Dr. P. Shurts returned to this Unit from 7 days leave in England.	
" "	29-5-16		11 horses railed to Base to-day from Candas Station & 1 mule Cpl Taylor & Pte T. Bedford.	
" "	30-5-16		Captain A. H. Foster. A.V.C. returned to this Unit from Leave in England. The following Ch & L/Cs and men of the Section have been appointed paid acting Lergts. for duty with 7th Divisional Artillery Units with effect from 5-5-16. No 33 Cpl. Singleton, No 45 Cpl. Lambert No 60 Private Taylor, No 65 Shoeing Smith Mi Chey, No 69 Private R. Baker, No 66 Private Bedford, No 39 Private Hopkins, No 22 Private Linton	

WAR DIARY
or
INTELLIGENCE SUMMARY.

Army Form C. 2118.

Place	Date	Hour	Summary of Events and Information	Remarks and references to Appendices
	31-5-16		Under authority of Local Corps Orders No 50 of 13-5-16. The following appointments have been made under authority of 1.D.D.V.S. 1st Army 4/690 of 18-5-16. No 17 Private J Heveringham to be Corporal 5-5-16. No 7 Private J Foster to be Corporal 5-5-16. No 33 Sergt. A Singleton A.V.C. attached 2 & 5 Brigade R.F.A. admitted Of. (W.R.) Field Ambulance.	[initials] Capt [initials] A.W. Foster Capt. A.V.C.

A.W. Foster
Capt. A.V.C.

O.C. 1/1 (W.R.) Mobile Veterinary Section

[Stamp: MOBILE VETERINARY SECTION * 49th (W.R.) DIVISION * Date 31-5-16]

Mob Vet C / Vol 10

WAR DIARY or INTELLIGENCE SUMMARY

Army Form C. 2118.

Place	Date	Hour	Summary of Events and Information	Remarks and references to Appendices
In the field	1-6-16		6 Horses railed to the base today from Landas Station i/c Sergt W.H. Linton A.V.C.	
" "	3-6-16	6.30 p.m.	Pay parade at 6-30 p.m.	
" "	5-6-16		9 Horses, 1 Mule (4 cases of suspected mange included) railed to the base today from Landas Station. i/c Sergt Lambert & Sergt R. Baker.	
" "	3-6-16		2/Lt F.J. Taylor proceeded to Head Quarters 147 Infantry Brigade at Marlenait, vice Lieut D. Greenwood, on leave	A/Lt Mosley
" "	8-6-16		8 Horse, 1 mule (1 case of suspected mange included) railed to Base today from Landas Station. i/c Sergt W.H. Linton.	Capt. J.C.
" "	9-6-16		Sergts Lambert Hopkin & Pte Heveringham Pte Clarkson A Batty Received Para Typhoid Inoculation	Capt. A.O.C.
" "	9-6-16		5 he feld R. destroyed and carcass sold in 20 francs to Monsieur Oscli Legroc. (M. Purulent tendo vaginitis with invasion of suffraginal coronal joint their hind leg.	
" "	12-6-16		9 horses (2 cases of mange included) railed to the Base from Landas station. i/c Sergt Hopkins & Pte Hardy	

WAR DIARY or INTELLIGENCE SUMMARY

Army Form C. 2118.

Place	Date	Hour	Summary of Events and Information	Remarks and references to Appendices
In the Field			Sergeants A.W.E. arrived as a draft from England and 7 were posted to Artillery Units. Sergt H. Arnold & E. Liff remained temporarily with M.V.S.	
" "	13.6.16		No 1/6 & 1/53 Sergts H. Haines and A. Liff A.W.E. were conducted to Headquarters 2.6.1. (Yk) Bde R.F.A. at Marennes by Sergt to C.E. Lambert & R. Baker.	
" "	13.6.16		Section teams were re-branded with foot numbers. 18 horses 2 mules (2 cars of suspected mange included) railed to Base from Candas Station.	
" "	16.6.16		The Section vacated Billets at Canaples. Billets were taken up at Miraumont — Ruitcourt — through Naours — Talmas — Ruhemvire. Ration Wagon Marched off at 8.30am Marched at 12 noon. (Sergt Lines in command) travelled with Unit.	
" "	16.6.16		Transport l/c Sergt Baker. No 6 Sergt H. & P.S. Taylor A.W.E. returned to their Unit.	
" "	17.6.16		Corporal Cooke & Pte Dunning returned to their Unit from the Base.	

WAR DIARY or INTELLIGENCE SUMMARY

Army Form C. 2118.

Place	Date	Hour	Summary of Events and Information	Remarks and references to Appendices
In Field	16/6/16		C.S. Limburg was on provided to Camp to the Sergt Taylor and brought forward Post for some time to Mirrawa.	
" "	17-6-16		Corporal G Cooke & Pte Dunning returned to this Unit to-day	
" "	19-6-16		7 tons 1 Mule (3 cases of Suspected Mange included) railed to Bond to-day from T-lewelleo Station. Sergt Taylor & Pte Unington included these cases were two very fine H.A. Horses from Hdy T Division - Suppurating Sandcrack & Rinc B.W. of Lorft (with exposure of pedal bone). The latter case was floated to station – Horses from Mirrawa (this few kilometres) N.B. the mention of the word "floated" has been omitted – it has been of great service & frequently used.	
" "	9-6-16		Information re death of Lord Kitchener & his Staff, when crossing to Russia through the "Hambelica" striking a mine was received with regret by all ranks. His loss is deeply felt but as the Zenith of his work + to his memory every one here everyone in the determination to do his bit and his duty, till we and our allies are Victorious.	

WAR DIARY
or
INTELLIGENCE SUMMARY

Army Form C. 2118.

Place	Date	Hour	Summary of Events and Information	Remarks and references to Appendices
Lulu Post	21/6/16		At Mirvaux Widening accommodation for 500 animals (quite good) at present have to supply 2000 emergency watering troughs all day. Sergt Taylor & Pte Knighton returned to this unit today.	A/G
	25/6/16		3 horses, 1 Mule, 2 cases suspected Mange included – railed to Base (Rouen) (es casus) today 1/c Sergt Bedford & Pte Farrar.	W.G
	26/6/16		13 horses & mules railed to Base today from MERICOURT Station i/c Sergt Hopkin Roe Stanley Thornly.	Foster
	28/6/16		Sergt Hopkin Roe Stanley Thornly returned to this unit.	
	29/6/16		RSPCA stores – Sharpening apparatus – Two Clipping Machines – R.S.P.C.A. Spray – (at Bridge) 1 Box cont. Saddlery 1 Bale Swords – 23 Horse Rugs – (at Bridge) Containing surplus Discarded Rations dumped at R.A. Dump at MIRVAUX.	Capt.
	2/7/16 5 p.m.		Orders received from E.O.E. R.A. to move to HEDAUVILLE.	
	1/7/16 a.m.		Marched off 8 a.m. – Transport & Capt Barker with M.I. detail/17 4. Arrived HEDAUVILLE 12 noon – Stabled & trained by 3 p.m. – on Englebelmer Road – all ranks are now in the open.	

T.134. W.L. W708—776. 500000. 4/16. Sir J.C. & S.

Army Form C. 2118.

WAR DIARY
or
INTELLIGENCE SUMMARY.
(Erase heading not required.)

Instructions regarding War Diaries and Intelligence Summaries are contained in F. S. Regs., Part II. and the Staff Manual respectively. Title pages will be prepared in manuscript.

Place	Date	Hour	Summary of Events and Information	Remarks and references to Appendices
Lahore field	18/6/16	3.30pm	G.O.C. Division visited lines & inspected unit at MIRVAUX. The General remarked on the excellent condition of the section horses.	A.M.S.
" " "	" "	6pm	A.D.V.S. Division visited lines & inspected unit.	Foster
	29/6/16		5 Horses railed to Base today from Advanced Station. 1/c Corporal G. Bostock.	
	30/6/16		No 80 Pte G. Burfield – 57. Pte E. Taylor – 93 Pte H. Portes – 48 Pte Hollioworth 29. Pte E. Collinson. 84 Pte S. Kitchen. 83 Pte E. Saylor. 85 Pte E. Banks. arrived as draft in the Eshew in the strength from today.	Capt
	30/6/16		Sergt Gambel Foster & 245 W.R. Bde R.F.A.	Pte
	"		" S. Tay McCaskey " " 246 " "	W.K.
	"		" Bedford Barker " " 249 " "	
	"		" H. Green Hinton " " 248 " "	
	20/6/16	10 am	Pay Parade	
	25/6/16		No. 6 Pte W.H. Pratt a.T.C. returned from School of Farriers nr Le Tréport. Certificate states that he is sufficiently thoroughly shoeing Smith & Farrier (or proficient as a cold shoer) is approved establishment of this unit with effect from 5/5/16. Authority A.V.S. Horse 4698 of 19/5/16.

T.134. Wt. W708—776. 500,000. 4/15. Sir J. C. & S.

WAR DIARY
INTELLIGENCE SUMMARY

Army Form C. 2118.

Place	Date	Hour	Summary of Events and Information	Remarks and references to Appendices
Lithefield	30/6/16		During the month the Unit has moved from Canaples to Mirvaux – Mirvaux to Hedauville – each time under orders of G.O.C. R.A. Patrols were sent out to render assistance to units having injured animals + to direct sick to M.V.S.	A/H/6 Foster Capt

A.N. Foster Capt AVC
Ey/m R.M.V.S.

MOBILE VETERINARY SECTION
49th (W.R.) DIVISION
No. date 30/6/16

Confidential
& Secret

A.G.
L.A.B.
B.G. Echelon
  the Base

Herewith War Diary for month
July 1916. for the Unit under
my command.

A. R. Foster Capt
  A.V.C.
Cdg 1/1 W.R.M.V.S.

49

1/W R Frost V.to/y Sec   Army Form C. 2118.

Vol 14

WAR DIARY
or
INTELLIGENCE SUMMARY.

Place	Date	Hour	Summary of Events and Information	Remarks and references to Appendices
Litlefield	1/4/16		Corporal L. Cooke returned to this unit from the Base today. It was omitted to record last month that the float had been invaluable – it saves many animals which would have been destroyed – it easily fills the place on the line of march of the L.G. limbered wagon for which it was exchanged. It should be stated that the float is easily drawn & a good pattern but most of poor material – the wood work is very faulty. The draft of 8 men which arrived on last day of last month appears to be good but they show an appalling want of training – they cannot ride – they know nothing about harness & its fitting – they know nothing about rifles – Most of them if not all were enlisted in the early part of 1915 – It certainly reflects on the Home Command that these men have not had one bit of training fit them for active service overseas. – there had been plenty of time & opportunity should have been made. –	A.W.S. Foster Capt. 1/4/16

Army Form C. 2118.

WAR DIARY
or
INTELLIGENCE SUMMARY.
(Erase heading not required.)

Instructions regarding War Diaries and Intelligence Summaries are contained in F.S. Regs., Part II. and the Staff Manual respectively. Title pages will be prepared in manuscript.

Place	Date	Hour	Summary of Events and Information	Remarks and references to Appendices
R. Ho Ft. 10a	2-7-16		In accordance with instructions from A.D.V.S. 49th Inf Division Private W.S. Darrand of this Section was detailed for duty at Advanced Veterinary Aid Post of 36th Division under Command of Lieut Shaw A.V.C. This Outpost is situated in Northumberland Avenue between Englebelmer and Mazlincourt. As our Division is in Reserve to 32nd & 36th Divisions very few of our animals are exposed to enemy fire but Lieut-Shaw has been offered any further assistance he deems it necessary to ask for.	
" "	3-7-16		11 Horses & Mules (Mare & Mange included) railed to Base to-day from ACHEUX Station i/c Sergt F. Baker & 8 Men of Foot & Loading Party.	
" "	4/7/16	10 a.m.	The 11 (Float) made journey to ACHEUX from HEDAUVILLE & also VARENNES to ACHEUX. Lieut. A.J. Heringham of this unit detailed to take over Advanced Post from 36th Division.	AJH

WAR DIARY or INTELLIGENCE SUMMARY

Army Form C. 2118.

Place	Date	Hour	Summary of Events and Information	Remarks and references to Appendices
Authuille	4/7/16	2p	O.C. took patrol Sgt Yates Ptes Dunning, Batty & Anbury Wood from Hedauville. Sgt Yates in the way helped Engineer detail to get to from whistle ditch – proceeded to the Bluffs over Black Horse Bridge to Leipschin Redoubt – Three mulbs – one sound – other 2 carefully wounded were found – collected – together with 2 Sgts Jacks-Reddy advanced (post vacated by 36' Division – if having been to was the brains of known for them to do so. Signal cases passed through five other ranks from 4. 8. M.V.S. reported for duty – conducting Pty of	
" " "	5/7/16		Sgts Baker & two men returned from Base today.	
" " "	6/4/16		23 Horses & Mules railed from A.C.HEUX to Corbaral Boyla 1 3 other ranks. – Boat made 4 journeys to A C.HEUX today.	
" " "	" " "	9a.m.	Arrived Post Ticked.	
" " "	" " "	noon	Sergt R. Rollo & 2 other ranks reported for duty – Nominal Rolls Co duties Rolls Sgt Parkes Ag Cpls – A.E.Boyle. M.G.Rule. Pte.Hartley Lundie K – Pickering G – Tiller A – Wells A – Witney – Winter C.	
" " "	6/4/16		3 other ranks detailed to conduct for Capten Player. – A.C.MUS.	

WAR DIARY
INTELLIGENCE SUMMARY

Army Form C. 2118.

Place	Date	Hour	Summary of Events and Information	Remarks and references to Appendices
Lithgow	7/9/16		5 Horses & Mules railed to Base today from A&NZ Sec. Sgt. Parker 1 Man - one case suffering from Ring worm & Scabies in isolation truck -	
"	" "		1 foal made 3 journeys to A.C.H.E U.K. B.L.R. Gold officers Charger destroyed today. Major Carson destroyed Patrol (Condemned Government) Perforation of Rectum caused by Shell splinter Castor and near Pozt.	
" " "	9/9/16		Corporal Boyle & 2 men returned to this Unit 8 inch. Ord Mules landed died on way to Base Sgt Parker & 7 men returned today Corporal Y & 3 men lent to C. & E. Mil. S. 3 men lent to G & 2 M.V.S.	
" " "	" " "		Mule stated in from I.V.A.R.L.O.Y. Twenty Horses & Mules - 2 cases of Mange included railed to Base	
" " "	10/9/16		from A.C.H.E U.K ½ H.B.S. Fawley - Pte Banks & 2 men of B.R. Forr animals railed to that station. One animal suddenly commenced to cough. Tracheotomy was necessary was performed before departure of train —	AH

WAR DIARY or INTELLIGENCE SUMMARY

Army Form C. 2118.

Place	Date	Hour	Summary of Events and Information	Remarks and references to Appendices
In the Field	10/4/16			
	11/4/16		4 Notices Boards to annexed Watering and Rest Pads. Dr. Desvignes this Morning from Harponville. Corpl. 173 man of 6 Pds.& 2 Field A.S Corps & 2 men returned from 4 B.M.V.S. D.T.R. Violet lines of cook. Water Cart Driver 72 mules reported for attachment to this unit. Pte Stephen JARVIS (3144) 1/6 East Riding Regiment (driver). 1/6 Jarvis & Pte Banks returned from Base. Sergt. A. Singleton reported today.	
	12/4/16		23 Horses. 3 Mules (2 cases of Mange included) railed to Base from ACHEUX by Corpl (BOYLE) R.F.A - 4 men - Corpl Boyle & 2 men will remain at Base.	
	13/4/16		Corpl Ride & 3 men returned from Base today to ACHEUX. Sgt Singleton posted to 2 & 5 Bde R.F.A. Road made 4 dumps	
	" "		Mounted horse from VARENNES into lines	
	" "		Horse noted from Rubempré twice By Cpl Yates - 16 Victualed VARENNES 20, horses 17 mules. Sept Pde 117 T.O.S.b 12 Ser. V.S with 152 Bde R.F.A. The 2 animals were taken over by 18. M.V.S. this Morning -	CMcGee

WAR DIARY
or
INTELLIGENCE SUMMARY.
(Erase heading not required.)

Army Form C. 2118.

Place	Date	Hour	Summary of Events and Information	Remarks and references to Appendices
Lillers	14/7/16		Corpl. Rule 13 men sent B.E. & 2. M.V.S. Sergt. Parker sent B.34 M.V.S.	
" "	15.7.16		A.D.V.S. visited Units.	
" "	" "		N° 3, Pte. HARDY. R. awarded Corps Pay at 4d rate (5 periods) with effect from 26-11-15.	
" "	" "		N° 26 Pte. BATLEY. G. was arrested for failure of 4 days pay for Corpl. Pay, for making an improper reply to N.C.O.	
" "			16 Horses 4 Mules (4 cases of Mange included) evacd. to Base today from A.6. HEUS ½, H.6. Fauly. Pte. ATKINSON Fowler Went one Journey to Station from Vaurenes to Units. A.D.V.S. visited Units.	
" "	17/7/16		E.S.V.E. Billet at Rueda. Horse Artillery Rueda in Units.	
" "	" "		OTC visited VARENNES Billet N° 19 Ott attack. Ex Horse Mule Horse Evacd. — Mule destroyed — Evacd Capt Milne.	
" "	18/7/16		12 Horses 2 Mules (3 cases of Mange included) evacd. to Base Other from A.6. H.E. Vet. Station & Corporal Rule. Ptes. Knighton & Tillers. Corpl. Rule & Pte Tillers will remain at this base then journey. Station & D.A.D.V.S. Reserve Army accompanied by A.D.V.S. visited Units today	
" "	" "			AWR

WAR DIARY
or
INTELLIGENCE SUMMARY.
(Erase heading not required.)

Army Form C. 2118.

Place	Date	Hour	Summary of Events and Information	Remarks and references to Appendices
Lutyford	18/7/16		Order Established O.C. 2 & 8 Bde. hors of course in extending privilege of men of 7 Bde. Canteen to A.V.C. personnel.	
" "	19/7/16		O.C. visited HARPONVILLE, no movement to have been left there by 36. D.T.C. inspected train Major not local Meuse have knowledge of them. O.C. visited Talmas. M.r H. Thullier started no horses left there Ap 24-6-16. Removed a days affort 3 & 50 paid. Pte Knighton returned from Base. Sgt. Parker & 2 men returned from 44 M.V.S. A.V.S. visited A.D.V.S. visited lines. 13 Horses (on Mange cases included) reated to Base from ALHEUX - Sgt Parker & 2 men about 3 on Mange Station.	
" "	20/7/16		N: WH. Turner V.S. reported. Capt Pike Sgt 1st S.B. Bulford cancelled - Reverted to permanent grade of Pte - Made a statement of complaint forwarded to A.D.V.S.	
" "	21/7/16		Patient Made Journey to Mesnil & the other local journey. Pte Turner A.V.C. O.Ns. Veterinary Hospital HAUTOE. 10 Horses 1 Mule	
" "	22/7/16		railed to Base today from ALHEUX i/c Sergt Parker 17 Men - Sergt Parker & 7 men returned to A.C. HEUX from Base Pte Tillen returned to Station - one horse from Varennes Line - 4 Horses Picketed to Station - One horse from Varennes Lines.	A.H.S.

WAR DIARY
or
INTELLIGENCE SUMMARY.
(Erase heading not required.)

Army Form C. 2118.

Place	Date	Hour	Summary of Events and Information	Remarks and references to Appendices
Yutkhull	23/9/16	10 am	C of E Parade Service in Cinema.	
		11 am	O.C. visited Advanced collected Tenres. Bag, Fabric Kits from ANDRIEUX. The Chateau (4 frames)	
	24/9/16		6 Horses visited Mules visited to Base from ACKHEUX. 2/Lt Bradley, Pte Callam 2 Suspected Mange 17 Remounts came in Ciudad. Sgt Pickard, Pte Pickering returned to the Unit. A.D.V.S. visited N. Irish Tea taken over (6 Squad) Issue holic area of Blount's & Auch HE Chateau visited attended Funeral also kecalated Mules arrived. No 3 Pte H Horlock to 1/3 W.R. field amb. M.G.G 9 men. Enlisting R.G. Sgt Tutin - Ptes W Cottar - T. Bowden A. Bonville - L. Rein A. T. Simmons - A. Gourvan - L.H. Bissell G O'Brien - M. Reynolds. reported today.	
	25/9/16	6 am	Motor trans: 6am. 10-11.5AM - 2-4.5 pm. A.D.V.S. visited lines Sgt Tutin Pte Bawden Reynolds sent to 1/1 S.M. MVS.	
			OC visiting the RISSART to horse shoeing by a.b left there by 5th Brahin Train R.E. 31 March/16. Collected 6,7 & 2 M.V.S. F Fd By 114 Res- Park - A.C.B.	A.W.G.

WAR DIARY or INTELLIGENCE SUMMARY

Army Form C. 2118.

(Erase heading not required.)

Place	Date	Hour	Summary of Events and Information	Remarks and references to Appendices
	25/7/16		N.Z. Horse left charge. Followed Yorks Dragoons. Takes over.	
	26/7/16		Engaged in lines all day. V. advanced post a miss. T/6 Bodley & Tillen returned today. Horse Mule collected from 3 London Field B. R.E. at Louvencourt. R.M. Shoot Mare died. Returns to following Gunshot. Shot Rib. Rural through spleen into Boreh. 13 horses to Muelo receive 6 Base /s 21/6/16 A.V.S. visited lines. 13 horses to Mulo reviled 6 Base /s 21/6/16 Tillen Pte O'Brien, Gowan - 3 cases of Mange included. L/Cpl Rohring - Pte Pam, Cutler Brooks - Schwein to H.S.M.M.S.	
	27/7/16		Remounts a joining to A.D.H.E.U.K. Sgt E.E. Hyatt applied to transfer - application cannot be considered SE 60830 Pte A Tillen SE 10516 " G. Pickering } Unfined 2 Corporals 24-7-16. No. 16 Pd/Cpl Sgt J. Haines } 97 " " " H. Senior Report rank of permanent graded Pte. 83 " " " E. Hara } Cpl Franklin - Pte M. Oakley - J. Wilson - J. Doyle - R. Wright awarded to L.Cp.	EHJ

WAR DIARY or INTELLIGENCE SUMMARY

Army Form C. 2118.

Place	Date	Hour	Summary of Events and Information	Remarks and references to Appendices
Lillers	28/7/16		A.D.V.S. visited lines.	
			27 H.q. horses collected from 49 W.R. Div. Train & entrained to N°2 Adv.: Remt Depot at Verille ℅ Cpl Franklin – Pte Wright – Pte Wilson. Dir la autorité R.R. a/c 5° 25/7/16 S.D.R. Bearer army. Pte Haines & Hare to N° 2 Veterinary Hospital Halve. Horses 1 Mule to Base from A.C.H. Étaples ℅ Sgt Tudor. Pte Bordelot. 93 Pte Gorlat returned to Strength (Complete)	
	29/7/16		1/Cpl Tickner 2 men returned from Base. 1/Cpl Pickering + men returned from Base. 16 3/E. Paraded Service in lines 10-30 a.m. 10 Horses 3 Mules to Base from A.C.H. Étaples ℅ 1/Cpl Pickering. 2 men – 2 cases of Mange to Remount included Strength Station. Pte Bordley	
	30/7/16 31/7/16		Sgt Tudor & 2 men returned from Base – Cpl Franklin & 3 men returned from Abbeville. Men returned from the months Return to establishment to form the main feature of the months.	

WAR DIARY
or
INTELLIGENCE SUMMARY

Army Form C. 2118.

advance post - i/c spr Corporal + 1 Pte - a second private being detailed each day to break from section to post to take charge of post which enforced taking turns. The Ptes are on patrol Staff the time so are always worn by the Patrol in advance dawn.

(2) The considerably large number of Genches examined to compare interior or exterior of this section. would of Genches Two animals have been destroyed at post - Hopeless cases   "   "   died at Section from Gunshot W'ds One Mule was destroyed at Section for Traumatic Pan arthritis of the Elbow - One Horse died from Abscess of Liver probably Tubercular.

31/7/16

C.W. Foster Capt: A.V.C.
Cdg: 1 W.R. M.V.S.

49

WAR DIARY or INTELLIGENCE SUMMARY
Army Form C. 2118.

Place: Puchevillers
Date: 1/8/16

O.C. - Sergeant Baker proceeded with Fleet to Outre bois - six miles beyond Doullens - to collect horse from Madame LAIGLE belonging to A Battery 71 Brigade R.F.A. Party returned to unit the following day - Horse well - Me Gieath (Rifleman wound of foot). PM about this*

Sergeant Yates visited M.M.A ordered horse into section - also visited 54 -
Field to R.E. collected - shot mule Mary.

*A return of Microscopic examination of Guns since received from M. Shoeing, M.R.C.V.S. Royal Veterinary College - Camden Town - London N.W. shows this there has been a case of Bacillary Neerosis -

Date: 2/8/16
L/Cpl Rickson + 2 men returned from the train. Advanced post upon a challenge last night - Corporal HEVENINGHAM given discretionary powers to move if necessary.

Date: 3/8/16
IN 97 Pte H. Senior sent to N°2 Veterinary Hospital HAVRE.
11 Horses + 6 cases of Mange included rated to Base from ACHEUX ½ Corporal Franklin - 1 man - it not made journey (station).
3 afh Mule Sally floated from 49 W.R. D.A. 6 times Destroyed on arrival

Hour: 11.0

Army Form C. 2118.

WAR DIARY or INTELLIGENCE SUMMARY.

Place	Date	Hour	Summary of Events and Information	Remarks and references to Appendices
	5/8/16		Suffering from Pan Ethric Ws. of Effort. O.C. visited Advanced Post. Sergt Baker visited H.Q. Staff. Resped showed 2 Horses Teeth. also Yorks Dragoons - a Squad admin'd Dose of Physic.	
	6/8/16		Corpl Franklin 17 Man returned from Base. C.of E. Parade Service in Lines. 10/45 a.m. Sergt Baker visited 15th Batty R.G.A. inspected horses report. A.D.V.S. visited Lines. O.C. visited Units.	
	7/8/16		27 Horses 1 Mule. (7 Mange included) 1/c Lloyd Killen 3 men railed to Base today. Road made to journeys toStation also for toda H.D. from 15th Batty R.G.A. from Varennes to Station. A.D.V.S. visited Lines. O.C. visited Units.	
	8/8/16 11 a.m		40 Horses collected from C/245 Batty. D/246 Batty R.F.A. nup of R246. Debility after influenza n-railed to Base ½ Sergt Turton ~5 men.	
	9/8/16 12 a.m		O.C. visited Out-Post - also Units 6 88 Sgt R. Parker SE 85.29 Pte O'Brien transferred 8TW6 M.V.S.	

T.134. Wt. W708—776. 500000. 4/15. Sir J.C. & S.

WAR DIARY
or
INTELLIGENCE SUMMARY.
(Erase heading not required.)

Army Form C. 2118.

Place	Date	Hour	Summary of Events and Information	Remarks and references to Appendices
Lilho	9/8/16		1/Cpl Tillen, Pte Pain, Barden, Oakley returned from Base.	
"	10/8/16		" " " Transferred to N'o M.V.S.	
"	11/8/16		8 Horses & mange included to Base % Capt Franklin & 1 man.	
			O.C. Visited units. Sgt Turton & 5 Men returned from the Base.	
			1/Cpl Pickering & 4 Men returned from 34 M.V.S. A.D.V.S. Visited lines	
			Pts E.L.G. Doyle - Gowan - transferred to N'o 6 M.V.S.	
	11/8/16		Surplus Stores returned to Base.	
	12/8/16		Corporal Franklin, 17 men returned from Base today - Pte Simmons	
			Bissell - Bowdler - Lenf & N'o 23 M.V.S. to remain at Base -	
			Hot Convoyed cad Gunshot from advanced post.	
			N'o 49 Pte A. Atkinson detailed as for today.	
	13/8/16		6.0 P.E Parade Service - lines.	
			A.D.V.S. Visited lines. O.C. Visited units -	
	14/8/16		Empty cases returned to Base - Packing cases -	
	15/8/16		12 horses - 5 Mules railed to Base % Capt Franklin, Pte Wright	
			Staines & Mango included, & Pte Franklin, Pte Wright to	
			remain at Base.	

WAR DIARY
or
INTELLIGENCE SUMMARY

(Erase heading not required.)

Place	Date	Hour	Summary of Events and Information	Remarks and references to Appendices
	13/6/16	9am	No.824. Pte S. Kitchen A.V.C. fell under his horse & broke his leg Tibia Fibula - admitted to 1/1 W. R. Field Amb. O.C. visited units - A.D.V.S. visited Unico. Pte H. Farrer returned from the Base.	
	14/6/16		A.D.V.S. visited M.V.S. - 7 horses 2 mules to Base 1/c Sgt Turton - 1 Man Sgt Turton to remained at the base.	
	15/6/16		No.29 Pte E. Gilkison No.31 Pte Hardy returned to this unit from F.P.No.1 Term of field punishment having expired.	
	16/6/16		Pte Bentle returned from Base today.	
	19/6/16		No.37 M.V.S. came into lower part of linas today. Mule Service Corps E. in linas 10/4.5 am	
	20/6/16		Seven horses 1 Mule (2 cases of Mange included) railed to Base from A.C.H.E. UX today. 1/c 2/6pl Bradley Pte Reynolds. Pte Reynolds to remain at Base. No.37 M.V.S. moved to adjoining field.	
	23/6/16		O.C. visited Units - A.D.V.S. visited linas ninspected horses. 2/6pl Bradley returned from Base -	

WAR DIARY
INTELLIGENCE SUMMARY
(Erase heading not required.)

Army Form C. 2118

Place	Date	Hour	Summary of Events and Information	Remarks and references to Appendices
In the field	24/6/16		14 Horses 3 Mules railed to Base 1/c Capt. Castle. Pte Hegley "Wilson" 3 Bases Mange included. Pte Wilson to remain at the Base.	
" "	25/6/16		Horses Made 2 Journeys to Station. Collected Droughts W. Delivery Regt.	
" "	26/6/16		Horses from 464 B.H.S.T.	
" "	27/6/16		Pte Savant withdrawn from Advanced Rd Station relieved by Pte Knighton. Capt Cooke Pte Hardy returned from the Base.	
" "	28/6/16		C of E Parade Service in lines. 10-45 a.m. 2/6th Fawley - Horse Made 2 Journeys to Station. 4 Horses one Mule railed to Base 1/c.	
" "			Say. Yates proceeded to Meerut Hosp the wounded horse undergoing treatment of Capt Pride once at A.D. Horse found to be suffering from fracture of Radius - destroyed immediately.	
" "	29/6/16		Horse made journey to Advanced Rd & Cavalry. Rd Mule Convoy O.C. visited units - 2/6th Fawley returned from Base - Reported that one animal died from Trypanitis on the way.	
" "	30/6/16		A.D.V.S. visited units - 11 horses 6 Mules railed to Base 1/c 1/6th Bradley 4 visited Mules - 1 Case Mange included. Horse Made 2 Journeys to Station.	
" "	31/6/16		Pte Say to Rollencourt	

Army Form C. 2118

WAR DIARY
or
INTELLIGENCE SUMMARY
(Erase heading not required.)

Place	Date	Hour	Summary of Events and Information	Remarks and references to Appendices
Dithfield	August		During the month O.C. has had charge of the following units - H.Q. & M.M.R. 49 W.R. Div - 49 W.R. Signal Co. R.E. a Squad Yorks Dragoons H.Q. 49 W.R. Div - R.E. - attendance to civilian wives at the Chateau has also been rendered on several occasions - Nothing has been done to increase the transport of the M.V.S. Representation has been made to A.D.V.S. Division & to D.V.S. Army - & if the S.S. (Supply wagon) travelled on the line of March with the Unit - an improvement would result - but in addition to present transport - a two wheeled vehicle - short draught - is needed by yours with the exception of Sgt Pickering - the Conducting Party has been returned to depot to its of origin - Sgt Pickering is retained until the deficiencies caused by the Returns being invalided.	

W.W. Foster Capt AVC
Colin W. Ennis

WAR DIARY or INTELLIGENCE SUMMARY

Army Form C. 2118

M+B Pet yseel 49

Place	Date	Hour	Summary of Events and Information	Remarks and references to Appendices
In the field	1-9-16		ADVS 49 (W.R.) Division visited lines	
" "	2-9-16		13 horses 1 mule. Railed to Base to-day c/c Corpl Cochete Bank & Clarkson. That made four journeys to station.	
	2-9-16		That proceeded to 464 Bay A.S.C. Leadvillers for Black Gold LD suffering from wound infected of foot.	
	2-9-16		ADVS visited lines	
	2-9-16		Corpl Hemmingham visited Divisional Dump Buckvillers and drew stores for A DVS Division and M.V.S.	
	3-9-16		That made four journeys to Advance Post for wounded horses	
	3-9-16		Sixteen horses one mule railed to Base to-day, I/C &/C Lawry Pte. Bowler & Binfield, that made four journey to station and detailed	
	4-9-16		A DVS visited lines after inspecting horses and detailed 8 Sergt to AVC from Home Station to Artillery Bello	
	4-9-16		Bay Geld LD destroyed fracture of knee bone (Gs-magnum)	
	4-9-16		OC accompanied ADVS to C/248 Batty R.F.A. and examined Bay Geld with Star fracture N. Shoulder. ADVS ordered the animal to be evacuated.	
	5-9-16		Bay mare H.D. 152 Hy Batty 9th Hd J floater from throning	

1875 Wt. W593/826 1,000,000 4/15 J.B.C. & A. A.D.S.S./Forms/C. 2118.

WAR DIARY
or
INTELLIGENCE SUMMARY

Army Form C. 2118

Place	Date	Hour	Summary of Events and Information	Remarks and references to Appendices
In the field	5-9-16		2.3 horses rode to day 1/c L/Cpl Pickering Pte Dunning-Barrett Banks & Collinson. One horse Suspected Mange incident Road made 3 journeys to station.	BMS
	6-9-16		Staff made one journey to Varennes and floated horse to the Acheux Station.	
	6-9-16		A.D.V.S visited lines.	
	7-9-16		A.D.V.S visited lines.	
	7-9-16		L/Cpl Fowler Pte Burfield and Fowler returned from the Base. L/Cpl Fawley reported that Bay mare belonging to 13th Batty R.F.A. 29th Division had her leg broken at Romes Camp owing to rough shunting. L/Cpl Fawley slightly injured.	
	8-9-16		No 21 Bay Gelding suffering from Pneumonia died 8-9-16. The animal belonged to 119 How Batty R.F.A. P.M revealed both lungs hepatised.	

Army Form C. 2118

WAR DIARY
or
INTELLIGENCE SUMMARY
(Erase heading not required.)

Place	Date	Hour	Summary of Events and Information	Remarks and references to Appendices
In the Field	8-9-16		OC under orders of the A.D.V.S. 49th (W.R.) Division visited Martinsart-Mesnil - Aveluy took horse returns and investigated Water supply in each place. Sgt Kenningham acted as guide. Full report rendered to A.D.V.S.	OWR
	8-9-16		19 horse one mule visited to base to day MB & I Epl Bradley, Pts Hallsworth & Hardy. Float made one journey to station and also made a horse belonging to Hdqrs 119 Hvy Batty R.G.A. and also made a journey to the Senlis Road Junction.	
	8-9-16		During the day several Balloons passed over the lines and dropt some literature (2) Gazette des Ardennes. These were picked up in in the W.R. Division.	
	8-9-16	6.50	handed to A.P.M. 49 (W.R.) Division. A.D.V.S. visited lines	

WAR DIARY
or
INTELLIGENCE SUMMARY
(Erase heading not required.)

Army Form C. 2118

Place	Date	Hour	Summary of Events and Information	Remarks and references to Appendices
In the Field	9-9-16		ADVS visited lines	
"	9-9-16		L/Cpl Behring Pte Banks Collinson and Dunning returned from the Base.	
"	10-9-16		A.D.V.S. visited lines and inspected horses.	
"	11-9-16		A.D.V.S. visited lines	
"	11-9-16		16 Horses railed to Base to-day. 1/c L/Cpl Cocker Pte Benfield 1 case of Ozoena included	
"	11-9-16		No.120 Bay Mare L.D. belong to C/247 Batt. R7a. died suffering from gun shot wound Belly	
"	11-9-16		L/Cpl Bradley Pte Hallowarth & Hardy returned to this Unit today. Heat made two Journeys to Station	
"	13-9-16		A.D.V.S visited lines and inspected horses	
"	13-9-16		Heat conveyed Horses from 148 M.G. Coy. to lines.	
"	13-9-16		Transport of men lent to 248 Bde. R7a. Horse Standings commenced	
"	12-9-16		OC visited Units & Advanced Post.	

WAR DIARY
or
INTELLIGENCE SUMMARY

(Erase heading not required.)

Army Form C. 2118

Place	Date	Hour	Summary of Events and Information	Remarks and references to Appendices
In the Field	14.9.16		32 Horses 1 Mule railed to Base to-day from Achew Station i/c 2/Cpl. Fawley. Pte Hardy - Collings - Darvand - Saylor 12 Cases of debility offrs. In/charge. 1 case of Broncho Pneumonia that made the journey to Station.	A.M.F.
" "	14.9.16		No 93 Pte H. Fowler admitted 1/3(WR) field Ambulance suffering from Bruised Pelvis and right groin	
" "	14.9.16		L/Cpl. G. Cooke & Pte Burfield returned to this Unit to-day	
" "	15.9.16		A.D.V.S. visited lines	
" "	16.9.16		A.D.V.S. visited lines and inspected Horses	
" "	16.9.16		24 Horses 2 Mules railed to Base to-day from Achew Station i/c L/Cpl. Pickering. Ptes Jarvis - Barthol & Halsworth.	
" "	16.9.16		No 93 Pte H. Fowler returned to this Unit from 1/3(WR) Field Ambulance to-day	
" "	16.9.16		2/Cpl. Fawley. Ptes Darvand Collings Hardy returned to this Unit.	

WAR DIARY
or
INTELLIGENCE SUMMARY

Army Form C. 2118

Place	Date	Hour	Summary of Events and Information	Remarks and references to Appendices
In Field	16.9.16		A.D.V.S. visited lines re 241 Bde R.F.A. Horses - Ordered them all to be tested with Mallein.	
" "	19.9.16		D.V.S. accompanied by D.D.V.S. Reserve Army - A.D.V.S. 4(a) Divn. A.D.V.S. 48th Divn visited lines and made inquiry re Horse Execution No 24 & 29 found to be glanders at Forqu-le-Eaux	
" "	18.9.16		5 Horses were tested with Mallein - No reaction.	
" "	18.9.16		11 Horses 1 Mule railed to Base to-day	
" "	18.9.16		No 31 Sergt C.E. & Yates proceeded to No 5 Veterinary Hospital for instruction re care and sharpening of Clippers Clipping Machine.	
" "	15.9.16		L/Cpl. Pickering Pte Banks Lewis & Hallsworth returned to their Unit to-day	
" "	16.9.16		Float made journey to Station	

WAR DIARY
or
INTELLIGENCE SUMMARY

Army Form C. 2118

Place	Date	Hour	Summary of Events and Information	Remarks and references to Appendices
In the Field	18/9/16		Parade for Pay	
" "	19/9/16		A.D.V.S visited and inspected lines to-day	
	20/9/16		C.E. visited Units.	
	20/9/16		1/Sgt. and one man returned from the Base.	
	21/9/16		Ten Horses two mules ordered to Base to day 1/C Sgt Booker Pte Hardy	
	21/9/16		A.D.V.S. visited lines	
	21/9/16		Short made journey to Treley Wood Stables horse to Section.	
	21/9/16		C.E visited Advanced Post and coopt 8 Royal Sussex Pioneers	
	22/9/16		C.E. visited units.	
	22/9/16		Horse floated from Advanced Post — destroyed — P.M. Compound Comminuted fracture of Cannon Off fore.	

WAR DIARY
or
INTELLIGENCE SUMMARY

Army Form C. 2118

Place	Date	Hour	Summary of Events and Information	Remarks and references to Appendices
In the Field	20.9.16		Pte Cooke returned from Base	
"	21.9.16		Float made journey to Advanced R.S.N	
"	22.9.16		No 29 Pte E Collinson admitted 1/2 (W.R.) Field Ambulance – Scalp wound – Fractures Tibia & Fibula and ribs. Accident 2.15 P.M died about five P.M. (In Ambulance) attended by Capt Adamson Lieut Anderson and Capt Adamson Lieut Anderson and D.A.C. M.C – Stretch off strength Strength.	MK
"	23.9.16		Stable construction commenced. Water Cart Mules and Pte Farries returned to 463 Coy A.S.C.	
"	24.9.16		C.C. i/c Detail Attend Burial Service at Lealvillers British Cemetery of Pte Collinson Chaplain Bragg Major Shawell	
"	24.9.16		Court of Enquiry in V.S times re circumstances causing death of Pte Collinson. President Capt Watson members Capt Buxton & Lieut Anderson	

WAR DIARY
or
INTELLIGENCE SUMMARY

Army Form C. 2118

Place	Date	Hour	Summary of Events and Information	Remarks and references to Appendices
In the Field	21.9.16		Witnesses Capt Foster Sergt Baker L/Cpl Bowley Pte Hallsworth & Dunning Lieut Whiteley R.A.M.C	WS
	21.9.16		A.D.V.S visited lines	
	23.9.16		Now under Administration of A.D.V.S 48th Division being attached to that formation	
	23.9.16		16 Horses two mules railed to Base 4/c L/Cpl Pickering Pte Hallsworth	
	25.9.16		C.O visited Advanced Park and Units also 8th Royal Sussex Pioneers.	
	25.9.16		A.D.V.S 18th Division visited lines	
	25.9.16		Float made three journeys to Station and floated one horse from 2/4 C Bde R.F.A Wagon-lines to section.	

WAR DIARY
or
INTELLIGENCE SUMMARY

Army Form C. 2118

Place	Date	Hour	Summary of Events and Information	Remarks and references to Appendices
In the field	25.9.16		ADVS 18th Division visited lines. C.E. took over the charge of the 41st R.F.A.	MF
	26.9.16		1 horse destroyed – Bay Geld Gangrenous Pneumonia. Grey Geld Emaciation Influenza.	
	26.9.16		C.E. visited field cashier.	
	27.9.16		C.E. visited two Batteries 41st R.F.A. base of suspected glanders at 19th Battery.	
	27.9.16		L/Cpl Pickering & Pte Hallsworth & Loyles returned from Base. Parade for Pay 8 to 9 A.M.	
	28.10.16		16 horses 1 mule railed to Base to day.	
	29.9.16		C.E. visited units, accompanied by ADVS 18th Division	

WAR DIARY
or
INTELLIGENCE SUMMARY
(Erase heading not required.)

Army Form C. 2118

Place	Date	Hour	Summary of Events and Information	Remarks and references to Appendices
In the field	30/9/16		O.C. visited advanced Post. O.C. visited 41st Bde H.Ft. 147th Batty. injected cholera vaccine inoculously with gallons 8 P.M.	
	30.9.16		Arranged with O.C. No 30 M.V.S. to take over advanced Post.	13th Division
	30.9.16		L/Cpl Zawley returned from the Base.	

A.N. Foster.
Capt - A.V.C.
Cdg. 1/1 W.D. m.v.s.

— 30-9-16.

Headquarters
49th (WR) Division

Re. D.R.O 2379 of 31-10-16

Herewith War Diary of 1/. (WR)
Mobile Veterinary Section for month
ending October 1916.

David Key
Capt~ AVC
Cdg. 1/. (WR) M.V.S.

2-11-16

WAR DIARY
or
INTELLIGENCE SUMMARY
Army Form C. 2118

Mob Katy See Vol 17

(Erase heading not required.)

Place	Date	Hour	Summary of Events and Information	Remarks and references to Appendices
Sin Sh. Z 1/11-10/11			Advanced Veterinary Ard Post handed over to 18th Division no 30 M.V.S. Cpl. Heveningham and Pte Knighton returned to section.	
" " "	2-1-16		30 horses two mules railed to Base to day from Achour Station i/c 2/Cpl Pickering Pte Hollowood Taylor 8 days. Took made one journey to station	A/S W.X.
" " "	3-1-16		Form Labelled Evacuation Roll - Consignment order - Telegram - handed over to O.C. No. 30 M.V.S. 18th Division for evacuation. Dupls to O.D.V.S. 18th Division	
	3-10-16		10 Sick horses handed to Cpl. Francis a/c of 50 M.V.S. 39th Division together with Timbrin - Were sitting etc for State consultation and 5 tents of Town Major Hedauville	

WAR DIARY or INTELLIGENCE SUMMARY

Army Form C. 2118

Place	Date	Hour	Summary of Events and Information	Remarks and references to Appendices
In the Field	3-10-16		R.A. orders to march off at 7am. Marched off 7-30am passed through Toeuville - Achicux - Marieux - Sarton - Infty Bn numerous halts. Drizzle for watering & feeding. Passed through Amplier and Outrebrille & shirted outlines & bivouacked for the night in an orchard between Milly and Marais See.	
" "	4-10-16		Marched off 9-45am. Passed through Milly - Brouches - Pommera close to Mondicourt through Belle Vue to La Bazeque Farm. Saw Town Major (Lieut- Wood 147 Infantry Bde) and letch up horse lines in field adjoining farm. Large hut allotted for men - tent allotted for N.C.O's - Armstrong hut for Officers. Both days have been wet but N.C.O's and them Lowe washed really hard and their conduct has been excellent during the two days march.	
" "	6-10-16		No 37 Sergt C.C. & to Yates ANTC returned to this Unit 5-10-16	
" "	6-10-16		2/Cpl. Pickering Post H. all wright - Saybo & Taylor returned to this Unit 5-10-16	
" "	6-10-16		OC visits units at Couturelle	
" "	7-10-16		O-C sent for by A.D.V.S. re Consolidated Return.	

WAR DIARY
or
INTELLIGENCE SUMMARY

(Erase heading not required.)

Army Form C. 2118

Place	Date	Hour	Summary of Events and Information	Remarks and references to Appendices
In Study	7-10-16		At 13085 Brown Marie R. 6yrs 15-2 Bay OH Paston 1/RFA Bradey found at morning Stables to have kicked - to be suffering from communicated fracture of Humerus. Destroy P.M. exam made.	
" "	8-10-16		Captain A.N. Forbes are admitted 1/2 (wd) Field Ambulance with fractured Tibia & Fibula accompanied by his servant No4 Pte P. Slothalex. Art. Captain A.H. Watson are took over the command of this Unit.	
" "	8-10-16		A.D.V.S. 49th (wd) Division visited & inspected the Section.	
" "	9-10-16		Drivers Cox & Sheller R.F.A. became attached to Section as Batmen to Captain A.H. Watson art.	
" "	9-10-16		No. 132 Pte A. Bowes A.V.C. arrived as a draft from England and was taken on the strength of this Unit.	
" "	12-10-16		13 am railed to base to-day from Saulty Station 1/c Corporal Booth & Pte Clarkson.	
" "	12-10-16		13110 Pte: Gedde R. (Pte Hardy) was evacuated to No. 22 Veterinary Hospital Abbeville suffering from Sesamoiditis O.F. Struck off Strength.	

WAR DIARY
or
INTELLIGENCE SUMMARY

Army Form C. 2118

Place	Date	Hour	Summary of Events and Information	Remarks and references to Appendices
In the field	13-10-16		Captain A.H. Walton A.V.C. acting A.D.V.S. of the Division during the absence of Lieut-Colonel A.W. Mason A.V.C. on leave in England.	
"	14-10-16		No 57 Pte E. Taylor A.V.C. was this day awarded 3 days C.B. and 3 extra night-guards for Conduct to the prejudice of good order & Military Discipline. Float made one journey to D.A.C. at Couturelle for 2 mules.	K.K.
"	15-10-16		No 15 Sergt. F. Baker A.V.C. entrained at Saulty Station for No 22 Veterinary Hospital Aubervill, there to resume duties as an instructor at the School of Farriery. Driver Shilton returned to his Unit and Pte T. Rattey A.V.C. was appointed Groom to Captain A.H. Walton A.V.C.	
"	16-10-16		24 horses 3 mules railed to Base to-day from Saulty Station I/c Sergt Baker. Pte's Knights - Bowles & Sayles. Float made two journeys to Station.	
"	17-10-16		Float made two journeys to Saulty. 1 to C/246 Bde R.F.A. (2) B/246 Bde R.F.A.	

WAR DIARY
or
INTELLIGENCE SUMMARY

Army Form C. 2118

Place	Date	Hour	Summary of Events and Information	Remarks and references to Appendices
In Billets	18.10.16		Pte Knighton – Banks – Saylor returned to the unit to-day	
- - -	" "		No 13106 Pte Newman R (Pte Batty) died. P.M. revealed Valvular Disease	
- - -	" "		Float made a journey to St Amand for Dr. Brown who was suffering from Bronchial Cold	
- - -	19.10.16		Horses & Mules railed to rear to-day from SAULTY Station ½ leave Fawley & Pte Taylor. Float made to journey to Station	
- - -	20.10.16		Black mare No. 1646 yrs Shortax No. N. Auratis FE taken seriously ill. Section to replace Pte Batty's Brown mare 6 C distributed Remounts for Saulty Station	BK
- - -	21.10.16		Corporal 69 Boothe temporarily attached to 148th Infantry Bde.	
- - -	22.10.16		Corporal A.G. Hemingham & two men proceeded to GRINCOURT and took our Billets & Stables from 1st to 2nd m.v.s. 17th Division	
- - -	22.10.16		Lieut. Colonel A.W. Mann and A.D.V.S. 49th Division returned from leave in England.	
- - -	23.10.16		14 Horses (mares) Suspected mange & 7 Influenza cases included railed to rear to-day from SAULTY Station & ½ lu Cpl. Pickering & Pte Saylor. Section made into new Billets at Grincourt. Excellent Stables for horses & good Billets for men.	

Army Form C. 2118.

WAR DIARY
or
INTELLIGENCE SUMMARY.
(Erase heading not required.)

Place	Date	Hour	Summary of Events and Information	Remarks and references to Appendices
K.K.1.W.	24.10.16		Lieut-Colonel A.W. Moon arr. A.D.V.S. HQ Eur Division visited and inspected Unit.	
"	25.10.16		No 4 Pte. E. Stockton arr. returned to the Unit from 43rd C.C.S.	
"	25.10.16		No 21 Pte. A. Kelley arr. taken on strength of Section pending further instructions from A.D.V.S.	
"	25.10.16		No 23 Pte. G. Knighton Cal. provided on leave to England. Leave granted from 26-10-16 to 4-11-16	
"	26.10.16		23 Horses 1 Mule railed to Base today from Saulty Station. i/c Lce.Cpl. Bradley & 3 men.	
"	26.10.16		Lce Cpl Pickering 1 man returned to this Unit.	
"	28.10.16		Captain A.H. Walton arr. provided on leave to England. Capt. D. Levi arr. acting O.C.	
"	29.10.16		Lce Cpl Bradley & 3 men returned to this Unit.	
"	31.10.16		23 Horses 6 cases of Mange included railed to Base today from Saulty Station. i/c Lce.Cpl. Fawley and 3 men. Float made 1 journey to Station	

31-10-16

Davie arr.
Capt. A.V.C.
A.v.C. (T.R.) O.C. Unit.

Army Form C. 2118.

WAR DIARY
or
INTELLIGENCE SUMMARY

Mob Vety Sec

Vol 18

(Erase heading not required.)

Place	Date	Hour	Summary of Events and Information	Remarks and references to Appendices
In the Field	2-11-16		2 F Horse 1 mule (10 cans of Mange included) railed to Base to-day from SAULTY Station i/c Lce Cpl Pickering & 3 men.	Office Records
	2-11-16		Lce Cpl. Fawley & 3 men returned to this Unit.	
	2-11-16		D.D.V.S. Third Army & A.D.V.S. 49(W.R.) Division visited ? inspected this Unit	
	5-11-16		Lce Cpl. Pickering & 3 men returned to this Unit 15-May	
	5-11-16		G.O.C. Division visited & inspected Section and expressed his appreciation of the work of the Section.	
	6-11-16		41 Horse (14 cans of mange included) railed to Base to-day from SAULTY Station i/c Lce Cpl Bradley Pts Atkinson, Lackson – Saylor – Hardy & Fowler.	
	6-11-16		A.D.V.S. Division visited the Section and inspected hands for evacuation	
	9-11-16		Captain Att Watson A.V.C. returned from leave in England and resumed Command of the Section.	
	9-11-16		Captain D. Keir A.V.C. proceeded on leave to England.	
	9-11-16		24 Horse (6 cans of Mange included) railed to Base to-day from SAULTY Station i/c Lce Cpl S Fowley & 3 men.	
	9-11-16		Sergt Mackay & Linton A.V.C. attached to Section pending further instructions from A.D.V.S. 49 (W.R) Division	

Army Form C. 2118.

WAR DIARY
or
INTELLIGENCE SUMMARY

(Erase heading not required.)

Place	Date	Hour	Summary of Events and Information	Remarks and references to Appendices
Le Havre	10.1.16		No. 23 Pte. J. Knights A.V.C. returned from leave in England.	
—	10.1.16		No. 1 Pte. W.H. Turner A.V.C. also reported for duty from No. 2 Veterinary Hospital Havre vice No. 4 Pte. G.E. Stoddart A.V.C. transferred to No. 2 Veterinary Hospital Havre. 11-1-16.	
—	10.1.16		Sergt. A.W. Mackey A.V.C. posted to 148 Infantry Bde vice Enfant G.J. who returned to Vet. Section.	
—	12.1.16		Captain A.C. Watson A.V.C. distributed Remounts at Warlincourt Station.	
—	13.1.16		A.D.V.S. Divn. visited Section and inspected Animals for evacuation.	
—	15.1.16		No. 16 Pte. J. Haines A.V.C. reported for duty from No. 2 Veterinary Hospital Havre vice No. 25 Pte. W.S. Dorrand A.V.C. transferred to No. 2 Veterinary Hospital Havre. 21 Horses (2 cases of Ringworm included) railed to Base to-day from WARLINCOURT Station.	
—	20.1.16		No. 122 Pte. T.B. Tennent A.V.C. (T) i/c Lu. 6th Pte. Pickering Pte. Hardy Pte. Bowes of the Northumbrian Army Veterinary Corps. reported for duty vice No. 31 Pte. R. Hardy A.V.C. transferred to No. 2 Veterinary Hospital. HAVRE.	
—	22.1.16			

Arthur Watson Captain

WAR DIARY or INTELLIGENCE SUMMARY

Army Form C. 2118.

Place	Date	Hour	Summary of Events and Information	Remarks and references to Appendices
In the Field	23/11/16		No 22 Sergt W/S Smiter Art. (T.F) transferred to No 2 Veterinary Hospital, HAVRE under instructions received from A.D.V.S. Division. Reverts to rank of unpaid acting Sergt art from 8-11-16 (Authority D.D.V.S. letter No V.149 of 7/16-11-16 (Field Army)	
	24/11/16		23 horses & 9 cases of Ringworm & 2 cases of Mange evacuated to Base today from WARLINCOURT Station i/c Lieut H. Bradley and 2 men.	
	25/11/16		Colonel A.J. Horninghams i/c and Drivers J. Cahill proceeded to Abbeville by road with unserviceable horse ambulance to be exchanged at No 5 Veterinary Hospital for one of a heavier type. Journey of 54 kilometers each way. 3 horses collected from Town Major at COUIN.	
	25/11/16		No 16 Pte J. Haines AVC admitted 1/3 (Ind) Field Ambulance suffering from acute Rheumatism.	
	27/11/16		22 horses & 3 mules railed to Base today from WARLINCOURT Station i/c 2/Lieut Bradley, Corporal Cooke & 3 men.	

Army Form C. 2118.

WAR DIARY
or
INTELLIGENCE SUMMARY

(Erase heading not required.)

Place	Date	Hour	Summary of Events and Information	Remarks and references to Appendices
27-11-16 to 30-11-16	30-11-16		Colonel A.F. Horringham are returned from Abbeville with Horse Ambulance E.S. exchanged at No 3 Veterinary hospital. 27 horses & mules (14 cases of mange & 3 cases of Ringworm) which railed to ran 5-day from WARLINCOURT Siding to 6th Troop C & mm.	

Arthur Watson
Capt. A.V.C.
A.D.V./ (2nd) mm.

30-11-16

Vol 19

SECRET.

WAR DIARY.

OF

1/1st (W.R.) Mobile Veterinary Section

FOR

December 1917.

WAR DIARY
INTELLIGENCE SUMMARY

(Erase heading not required.)

Army Form C. 2118.

Place	Date	Hour	Summary of Events and Information	Remarks and references to Appendices
In the Field	2-12-1916		Float made journeys to SOUASTRE (2) and one journey to PAS	
	"		A.D.V.S. of the Division visited the Section	
	3-12-1916		Float made two journeys - one to GUADIEMPRE - one to ST AMAND	
	"		Sergt Yates in charge of Escort (Pte Jennings) entrained for ABBEVILLE there to report to A.P.M. to escort the prisoner, namely:- No 33 Pte (Lc Cpl) Fawley W.V.C. - No 1 Pte WM Thorne R.G.E.	
	4-12-1916		Float made two journeys to WARLENCOURT Station	
	"		28 Horses and 5 Mules (4 cases of Mange included) were routed to Base today from WARLENCOURT Station - Lt Cpt. Pickering and 2 men in charge	
	5-12-1916		Float made one journey to ST AMAND	
	"		I.C. with Corporal Heringham visited lines of 46th North Midland Mobile Veterinary Section at MARAIS-LE-SEC - and made arrangements to take over Billets from them on 6-12-1916	

WAR DIARY or INTELLIGENCE SUMMARY

Army Form C. 2118.

Place	Date	Hour	Summary of Events and Information	Remarks and references to Appendices
In the Field	5-12-1916		Sergt Yates and Escort returned from ABBEVILLE.	
	6-12-1916		The Section orderd Billets at GRINCOURT and marched to MARAIS-LE-SEC, and there to go into the Billets of the 46th M.V.S. - Stables available for Horses for one night only	
	7-12-1916		No 53 Pte (L.Cpl) Fawley reverted to rank of Private. Twice Drunkenness in ABBEVILLE - No. 1. Pte 204 Turner L. M.C. awarded 4days Field Punishment No 1 :- crime Drunkenness in ABBEVILLE.	
	"		Horse proceeded to HENU and from there removed the office of the A.D.V.S. to LUCHEUX, and also Hunted Horse in from LUCHEUX L.Cpl Bradley in charge.	
	10-12-1916		Start made journey to BOUQUEMAISON for Horse belonging to 464 Coy A.S.C.	
	"		22 Horses (2 cases of Mange included) were railed to Base to-day from DOULLENS Station - L.Cpl Bradley and 2 men in charge	

Army Form C. 2118.

WAR DIARY
or
INTELLIGENCE SUMMARY

(Erase heading not required.)

Instructions regarding War Diaries and Intelligence Summaries are contained in F. S. Regs., Part II. and the Staff Manual respectively. Title Pages will be prepared in manuscript.

Place	Date	Hour	Summary of Events and Information	Remarks and references to Appendices
In the Field	9/12/16		The O.C. visited MEZEROLLES and collected the undermentioned animals which had been left owing to sickness:—	
			1 L.D from M. PETIT - MEZEROLLES	
			5 L.Ds from Mme VITRY - MEZEROLLES	
			1 L.D from M. PRONIER - MOULIN-DE-COURCELLES	
			1 L.D left with M. PETIT - BARLEY was destroyed by orders of the O.C.	
			1 Shoot Geld. was collected to-day from M. OSSET LEFEBRE	
	10/12/16		The O.C. visited AMPLIER and collected from LE MAIRE of AMPLIER the undermentioned animals which had been left by the 14th Bn R.F.A, being unfit to travel:—	
			1 L.D. Roan Geld - 1 L.D Bay Mare	
	10/12/1916		The O.C. visited and collected the undermentioned animals which had been left unfit to travel.	
			1 R. Shoot Geld - 1 L.D Shoot Geld also from M. H·GUFFIN - AMPLIER - 1 Bay Geld L.D	

WAR DIARY
INTELLIGENCE SUMMARY

(Erase heading not required.)

Army Form C. 2118.

Place	Date	Hour	Summary of Events and Information	Remarks and references to Appendices
In the Field	18-12-1916		Hunt made journey to MEZEROLLES for a Horse.	
"	16-12-1916		No 14 Corporal A.G. Hunningham promoted to rank of Paid Acting Sergeant from 24-10-1916 to complete Establishment :- Authority Corps Orders No. 59 of 12-12-1916.	
"			No 6 L/Corporal from M.M.S. BRAILEY becomes - 1 Day n.m.e. L/C. Eyles 23rd D.A.C. No 6 Lance Corporal Bradley promoted to rank of Corporal.	
"			Bay mule Gelt belonging to 2/Tabular D.A.C (14606) was destroyed, Post Mortem examination was performed by the V.O.	
18-12-1916			14 Horses and 2 Mules were railed to base to be sent from DOULLENS Station. Corporal Cooke and two men in charge.	
"			The J.D. Vet accompanied by the D.A.A.Q.M.G. and the O.C. visited the Horse Lines and Billets and held a consultation.	
"			No 23 Pte J Knighton promoted to rank of Unpaid Acting Lance Corporal.	
"	19-12-1916		Hunt made one journey to LUCHEUX for a Horse.	
"			Hunt made one journey to C ROUCHES	

Army Form C. 2118.

WAR DIARY
or
INTELLIGENCE SUMMARY
(Erase heading not required.)

Instructions regarding War Diaries and Intelligence Summaries are contained in F. S. Regs., Part II. and the Staff Manual respectively. Title Pages will be prepared in manuscript.

Place	Date	Hour	Summary of Events and Information	Remarks and references to Appendices
In the Field	19.12 1916		The O.C. visited and collected from M LEROUX - LE MAIRE of NEUVILLETTE the undermentioned animals left by the 9th Reserve Park R.D.C. unfit to travel. 1. L.D. Short Geld. 2. H.D. Chestnut Geld. 3. L.D. Bay Geld.	
	19.12 1916		The O.C. visited and collected from M LEGRIS JOSEPH - MEZEROLLES the undermentioned animals, which had been left by 10th Res Park R.T.A. also 1. Bay Geld L.D. 2. Dark Bay Geld L.D. One horse was found unfit to travel and was destroyed by O.C.'s orders.	
	20.12 1916		11 Horses - through Exams were railed to-day from BOUQUEMAISON Station to Pare. 2 men in charge. 14 Horses and 2 Mules were railed to Pare to-day from DOULLENS Station - Lt. Col Knighton and 1 man in charge.	
	21.12 /16		Sergt. Yates forwarded to FROHEN-LE-GRANDE and collected from M TEMPEZ CLAIRE - 1 Bay Short Geld - which had been left by 37th D.A.C. unfit to travel.	

Army Form C. 2118.

WAR DIARY
or
INTELLIGENCE SUMMARY

(Erase heading not required.)

Instructions regarding War Diaries and Intelligence Summaries are contained in F. S. Regs., Part II. and the Staff Manual respectively. Title Pages will be prepared in manuscript.

Place	Date	Hour	Summary of Events and Information	Remarks and references to Appendices
In the Field	20/12 1916		Shoeing Smith W.H. Pratt A.V.C. proceeded to England on 10 days leave of absence – Returning 31-12-1916.	
	22/12 1916		117 Pvt. Acting Sergeant W.J. Bothwell A.V.C. reported to O.C. to duty from Base Section D.A.B. to be sent to No. 2 Base Veterinary Hospital – HAVRE as Private – Authority D.D.V.S. 3rd Army	
	23/12 1916		193 Pvt. Acting Sergeant J.E. Wallin A.V.C. reported to O.C. to duty from 4th Section D.A.B. to be sent to No. 2 Base Veterinary Hospital – HAVRE as Private Acting Sergeant – Authority D.D.V.S. 3rd Army	
	"		193 Sergeant Acting Sergeant J.E. Wallin and 117 Pte. W.J. Bothwell proceeded to No. 2 Base Veterinary Hospital – HAVRE, as per instructions	
	25/12 1916		The N.C.O.'s and men of the Unit were entertained to Christmas Dinner by the O.C. at the CAFE DUMARAIS Sec-A-DOULLENS to day	
	"		No. 8 Pte. J. Downing A.V.C. promoted to rank of Unpaid Acting Lance Corporal to day	

WAR DIARY
or
INTELLIGENCE SUMMARY

Army Form C. 2118.

Place	Date	Hour	Summary of Events and Information	Remarks and references to Appendices
In the Field	28-12 1916		44 Horses and 2 Mules (8 cases of Mange enclosed) were railed to Base to-day from DOULLENS Station - Lt. Col. Pickering and 5 men in charge	
	"		42 Horses all Mange Cases were railed to Base to-day from BOUQUEMAISON Station - Corporal Cork and 4 men in charge No. 6	
	29-12 1916		Corpl Brundley R.V.C. proceeded to England on leave to-day returning 9-1-1917.	
	30-12 1916		4 Horses - Mange Cases were railed to Base to-day from DOULLENS Station - Lt. Col. Knightlen in charge.	

Arthur H Watson
Captain R.V.C.
C.O. V.R. Mobile Veterinary Section

Vol 20

SECRET.

WAR DIARY.

OF

Mobile Vet. Sect. Hq^th (WR) Division

FOR

January 1917.

Army Form C. 2118.

WAR DIARY
or
INTELLIGENCE SUMMARY
(Erase heading not required.)

Place	Date	Hour	Summary of Events and Information	Remarks and references to Appendices
In the Field	1-1-19		20 Horses and 4 Mules (16 cases of Mange) were railed to Base to-day from DOULLENS Station. Le/Cpl Browning and 2 men in charge	
	2-1-19		The O.C. visited FROHEN-LE-GRANDE with reference to a horse left by 103 Bde. R.F.A.	
			Have proceeded to MENDICOURT to fetch horse belonging to 148 Infantry Bde.	
	3-1-19		No. 48 Pte. F. Hollowith A.V.C. awarded 7 days Field Punishment No.1. Crime:- was talking to obey an order. Field Forge received to-day	
			No. 132 Pte. A. Bowes proceeded to FROHEN-LE-GRANDE to collect a horse left by 103 Bde. R.F.A.	
	4-1-19		No. 48 Pte. F. Hollowith proceeded to 1 P.M. 49th D.V. Divn to perform 7 days Field Punishment No.1.	
			Have proceeded to LUCHEUX to fetch a horse.	
			36 Horse and 3 Mules (24 cases of Mange included) were railed to Base to-day from Doullens Station. Le/Cpl Pickering and 4 men in charge	

Army Form C. 2118.

WAR DIARY
or
INTELLIGENCE SUMMARY
(Erase heading not required.)

Instructions regarding War Diaries and Intelligence Summaries are contained in F. S. Regs., Part II. and the Staff Manual respectively. Title Pages will be prepared in manuscript.

Place	Date	Hour	Summary of Events and Information	Remarks and references to Appendices
In the Field	6-1-17		32 Horses/Mules Cases were handed to Base to-day from BOUQUEMAISON Station. Cpl Cook & 2 men in charge	E.M.L.
	"		4 Horses and 1 Mule (2 Cases of Scabies included) were railed to Base to-day from DOULLENS Station. L. Cpl Knighton and 1 man in charge	
	7-1-17		L. Cpl Denning and Driver Slew proceeded to LUCHEUX and removed office of A.D.V.S. to BAVINCOURT	
	8-1-17		Went proceded to COURTERELLE to bring in horse belonging to B/Echelon 4gth (?) D.A.C. L. Cpl Pickering in charge	
	9-1-17		41 Horses and 2 Mules (36 Cases of Mange included) were railed to Base to-day from BOUQUEMAISON Station. L. Cpl Pickering and 5 men in charge	
	"		Escort (L. Cpl Denning) proceeded to BAVINCOURT to fetch No. 46 Pte F Hallsworth A.V.C. from A Pk 29th Div'n - on completion of 7 days Field Punishment No. 1.	
	10-1-17		No. 57 Pte E F Taylor A.V.C. proceeded to 1 D.V.S. 30th Div'n for Musical Examination	
	10-1-17		Went proceeded to OEUOCHES to collect horse belonging to R.245 Bde R.F.A.	
	11-1-17		Went proceeded to OEUOCHES to collect horse belonging to 312 Bde R.F.A. 62nd Div'n	
	12-1-17		Went proceeded to OEUOCHES to collect horse belonging to 62nd Div'n	

Army Form C. 2118.

WAR DIARY or INTELLIGENCE SUMMARY

(Erase heading not required.)

Place	Date	Hour	Summary of Events and Information	Remarks and references to Appendices
In the Field	13-4-17		30 horses and 2 Mules, all Mange cases were railed to Bruex to-day from DOULLENS Station. L/Cpl Dunning and 3 men in charge	
	"		No 51 Pte E.R. Taylor A.V.C. proceeded to HAVRE - to report to O.C. No 2 Base Veterinary Hospital as per Authority of A.D.V.S. 30th Division - proceeded by Railway train from DOULLENS Station. Have made two journeys to LUCHEUX for horses belonging to A/245 Bde. R.F.A.	
	14-4-17		30 horses and 2 mules (24 cases of Mange included) were railed to Bruex to-day from DOULLENS Station. Cpl Bradley and 6 men in charge	
	"		A.D.V.S. 30th Division visited the Shelters and inspected 93 cases of Mange and Inspected Mange. He ordered 44 to be destroyed and 49 to be returned to their units.	
	15-4-17		The O.C. and Sergt Huningham visited SAULTY - LARBRET and inspected Stabling and Billets - Preparatory to taking same over 16-4-17.	
	16-4-17		The Section vacated Billets at MARAIS-LE-SEC - A - DOULLENS and marched to SAULTY - LARBRET, and took over Billets of the 40th M.V.S. 30th Division, also took over 34 horses and 2 Mules - 25 cases of Mange included	

2449 Wt. W14957/M90 750,000 1/16 J.B.C. & A. Forms/C.2118/12.

WAR DIARY
or
INTELLIGENCE SUMMARY

Army Form C. 2118.

Place	Date	Hour	Summary of Events and Information	Remarks and references to Appendices
In the Field	18-1-17		56 Horses and 4 Mules (45 tours of Mange included) were railed to Brac to-day from SAULTY Station. L/Cpl Houghton and groom no change	
	19-1-17		No 16 Pte Hames A.B.C. was admitted by 2/1 208 Field Ambulance to-day & **subsequently discharged from hospital 20-1-17**. The A.D.V.S. 49th Division visited the Section and inspected stables and horse lines.	HFG
			9 Horses - cases of Mange admitted to Section to-day 1 Horse was evacuated to the Stables last to-day.	
	21-1-17		Farr - Corporal Knighton & 7 men returned from the Base.	
	22-1-17		A.D.V.S. 49(W.R) Division visited and inspected Sick Animals.	
	22-1-17		Box Respirators issued to Officers N.C.O's and men. Instructions in the use of the Box Respirator were given by Lieutenant Francis.	
			Town Major L'ARBRET.	
	23-1-17		Captain Arthurs A.V.C under orders of A.D.V.S. Division took over command of this unit from Captain A.H Watson A.V.C relieved.	
	23-1-17		A.D.V.S accompanied to Captain Forbes.	
			27 Horses (19 cases of Mange included) railed to Base to-day from SAULTY Station i/c 6/R Cooke	

Army Form C. 2118.

WAR DIARY
or
INTELLIGENCE SUMMARY

(Erase heading not required.)

Instructions regarding War Diaries and Intelligence Summaries are contained in F.S. Regs., Part II. and the Staff Manual respectively. Title Pages will be prepared in manuscript.

Place	Date	Hour	Summary of Events and Information	Remarks and references to Appendices
X Ostrold	24-1-17		Animals entrained at Saulty Station for No 22 Veterinary Hospital Abbeville on 23-1-17 left Railhead on 24-1-17.	
—	24-1-17		Two equine carcases buried behind and properly buried in the brick yard field.	
—	24-1-17		A.D.V.S. 49 (WR) DIVISION visits Section	
—	25-1-17		Medical inspection of all ranks for Scabies by Major Peck. D.S.O.	
—	26-1-17		Sick horse in the Mange Section dropped dead 7-30 p.m.	
—	27-1-17		Corporal Cooke & Party returned from the Bar 5 a.m.	
—	27-1-17		Village shelled for an hour and a half. One Army Service Corps driver wounded, 1 civilian killed and several wounded – houses destroyed and road damaged. Retaliation by heavy guns effective. An Post-mortem on Bay mare +D (dropped dead of Mange Section on 26-1-17) revealed Pleuro-Pneumonia of about 3 weeks standing	
—	27-1-17		Heat wounded 1/c Serg't old 1st evening hour and to No 2 Q.C.S. to pick up a Rehmont with fracture. The animal was immediately destroyed and conveyed to L'ARBRET Brickyard for burial by A.S.C.	

2449 Wt. W14957/M90 750,000 1/16 J.B.C. & A. Forms/C.2118/12.

WAR DIARY or INTELLIGENCE SUMMARY

Army Form C. 2118.

Place	Date	Hour	Summary of Events and Information	Remarks and references to Appendices
In Stables	28-1-17		C. of E. Communion Service in Billet of O.C. 11am Major Barnes C.F. A.D.V.S. visited and inspected horses. Bay mare No 46 destroyed by order of the A.D.V.S. suffering from Suspected mange-Debility and old age.	
	29-1-17		O.C. NCO's and men of the Section paraded and received instruction in the use of the Box Nosphrator and went through a Gas Tent. All Respirators fitted well and were efficient. 35 Horses (9 cases of mange included) railed to Base to-day from SAULTY Station i/c Cpl C. Bradley Pts Clarkson Burfield Tennit & Sayles.	
	31-1-17		Drag-Shoe fitted to 7 Cart on the recommendation of O.C. 4g (iw2) Divisional Train It is doubtful if it is a wise plan to put a drag-shoe on a list wheeled vehicle.	
	30-1-17		During the month the weather has been extremely severe almost continuous frost and Snow. Influenza and Catarrhal Sore Throat has effected most of the Section.	

A.W. Foster
Capt-a.v.
O.C. 4.g.(iw2) m.v.s.

SECRET.

WAR DIARY.

OF

FOR 1917.

No 21

SECRET.

WAR DIARY.

OF

1/1 (W.R.) Mobile Veterinary Sect.

FOR

February 1917.

WAR DIARY or INTELLIGENCE SUMMARY

Army Form C. 2118.

Place	Date	Hour	Summary of Events and Information	Remarks and references to Appendices
In the Field	1-2-17		35 Horses railed to-day from Sailly Station. 1/c Corporal Bradley. Pte Clarkson - Burfield - Tennant & Sayles (19 Cases of Mange included) Pte Sayles had to return to Unit on account of illness.	
" "	2-2-17		O.C. attended lecture on "Censorship" at BAILLEULMONT.	
" "	3-2-17		Lieut-Colonel A.W. Moran arr. from A.D.V.S. 49(W.R) DIVISION proceeded on leave to England, Captain A.N. Jones act acting A.D.V.S. division In accordance with Army Council Instruction No 2188 of 1916 all Army Veterinary Corps (Territorial force) have been promoted to the Royal Army Veterinary Corps from 1-12-1916. New lists for the duration of War from 1-12-1916. Have to-day number allotment of NCOs add men of this Unit.	
" "	4-2-17		Corporal Bradley & Ptes Clarkson - Tennant & Burfield returned from France to-day. No 132 Pte Bowes admitted 1/1 (WR) Field Ambulance.	
" "	5-2-17		Acting A.D.V.S. accompanied D.D.V.S. Third Army inspecting 150 Pdk Army T.A. also A.S.C Battns 246 (W.R) Brigade R.F.A	

WAR DIARY or **INTELLIGENCE SUMMARY**

Army Form C. 2118.

No R Middlesex Regt Section

Place	Date	Hour	Summary of Events and Information	Remarks and references to Appendices
Victoria	6.2.17		Section vacated Billet No 21 at LARBRET which was taken over by 40th Mns. 30th Division. Marched off 10am arrived HUMBERCAMP 11-30am and took over horse lines on LABAZEQUE Road – care and standings for Sickson horse & Surgical & Medical cases. All infectious cases in the open. Rugs removed from all horses under care.	a.M.F.
" "	7.2.17		Water cart attached to this Unit to draw water from LABAZEQUE CHATEAU owing to HUMBERCAMP supply system being entirely frozen up.	
" "	7.2.17	6-30pm	Pay Parade at Billet of O.C. (No 52)	
" "	7.2.17		SE/ No 4436 Pte W HODGKINS arrived as a reinforcement from No 2 Veterinary Hospital HAVRE and is taken on the strength of this Unit – from 7 – 2 – 17.	
" "	8.2.17		2 Horses & 2 Mules railed to Base from South Station 1/C 2nd Cpl. Knighton – Pte Hallworth – Supplied. 5 qrs of Blankets & Blitter 9 cans of Mange – 3 cans of hie 1 can of Strange.	

2449 Wt. W14957/M90 750,000 1/16 J.B.C. & A. Forms/C.2118/12.

WAR DIARY or INTELLIGENCE SUMMARY

Army Form C. 2118.

X1 W.R. Mobile Veterinary Section

Remarks: A.M.F.

Place	Date	Hour	Summary of Events and Information
In the Field	8-2-17		S.E. No 10516 Pte Ore(?) BW) & Pickering A.V.C. proceeded on leave to England. Leave granted from 9-2-17 to 19-2-17.
" "	9-2-17		Acting ADVS accompanied DDVS Third Army inspecting D.A.C. Batteries of 2, 246 Bde R.F.A. C B and A Batty 245 Bde R.F.A. D/246 Shoeing Bad. C/246 Grooming very bad. C/245 Horses finding but appear in good condition – complain unable to get them shorn. B/245 Shoeing ? Many cases of mange. A/246 Grooming bad. 70 Horses 3 Mules (48 cases of Mange & 1 case of Ulceration (Syphilis mallein)) railed to Rouen to-day from SAULTY Station i/c Corporal Cooke & 8 men 1 NCO and 12 men of the R.F.A. assisted with the entraining of the animals at the Station.
" "	15-2-17		No T.T.08238 Pte Fowler H. A.V.C. proceeded as one of the escorting Party to ABBEVILLE thence to proceed by Rail to HAVRE en route thence to No. 2 Base Veterinary Hospital for return to England on account of being claimed by his parents for under age.

WAR DIARY or INTELLIGENCE SUMMARY

Army Form C. 2118.

1 XIII-R. Mobile Veterinary Section

Place	Date	Hour	Summary of Events and Information	Remarks and references to Appendices
Field	17-2-17		OC accompanied by Sergt-A.J. Hemingham visited lines of the 2(WR) Field Ambulance at LA CAUCHIE and examined Bay Mare suffering from fracture off Tibia. Animal destroyed by Sergt Hemingham with permission of the OC.	A.M.I.
" "	19-2-17		Float made one journey to to Bargue Chateau and collected one horse from 463 Bay QSC. suffering from Abscess Thigh. Pay Parade at Billet 9 O.C. 2 p.m.	
" "	21-2-17		The following men have been awarded "Good Conduct Badges" on completing a term of good conduct at the date stated against their names. No. T.T.03165 Pte Farrer tt. 13/11/16. No 4436 Pte Hodgkins W. 26/1/17.	
" "	22-2-17		118 Horses 1 mule (83 cars of manje inclded) railed to B.pe to-day from South Slater I/c Coporal Bradley act. and Conducting Party of 1 NCO. and 16 men from Divisional Royal Netting. Float made two journeys to station. Float Cart to Captn Smithes act. to Float-Sub Hors from Mondicourt to SEMRS. at GROUCHES	
" "	23-2-17			

WAR DIARY or INTELLIGENCE SUMMARY

Army Form C. 2118.

X W.R. Mobile Veterinary Section

Place	Date	Hour	Summary of Events and Information	Remarks and references to Appendices
Bellacourt	23.2.17		Sergt. Yates and 2 O.R. proceeded to LUCHEUX to obtain Billets for this Unit for L/Cpl "C" 2 O.J. and L/Cpl G. Pickering A.V.C. returned from leave in England.	
" "	24.2.17		36 Horses 17 mules railed to Base to-day from SAULTY Station i/c L/Cpl.	
" "	25.2.17		Drivers and 8 men of 150 Bde Army F.A. 2 from each Batt. Water Cart taken over by this Unit also one t/r of harness A.S.C. converted Water Cart taken over to act as driver. Pte Hallsworth detailed to act as driver.	
" "	25.2.17	1.17 p.m.	Sergt yates proceeded to Halting Place for 26th int i/c Pte Tawley and Pte Hallsworth and took Water Cart.	
" "	26.2.17	10 a.m.	Moved off from HUMBERCAMP owing to state of roads had to proceed via Rabelière instead of straight on past LABAZIQUE FARM - March very much impeded by Horse Ambulance - LUCHEUX reached about 3.6 p.m. - Billets taken up at LA FOLIE FARM. alongside A/246 W.R. Bn. R.F.A. Horses & vehicles - also two rooms	
" "	27/2/17		Day spent in cleaning saddlery, Harness & Vehicles wheels obtained from H.Q. W.R.D.A.C. at GROUCHES for Horse Ambulance. Horse 07/5 4th Regt- met in LUCHEUX too lame to travel. On Examination	
" "	" "	11 am	foot - protruding shoeing Smith of 249 W.R. Sig Coy	

Army Form C. 2118.

WAR DIARY or INTELLIGENCE SUMMARY

X/W R Mob Veterinary Section

(Erase heading not required.)

Place	Date	Hour	Summary of Events and Information	Remarks and references to Appendices
In the field	27/1/19	4 P.M.	Horse to finite S/Batn 293 Pde. Army F.A. in LUCHEUX — Tour Major LUCHEUX – A.D.V.S. 1st W.R. Div – Notified absence V.O. Capt Jordan A.V.C. re the horse's sent memo to D.G. 1/5 Yr Regt.	
" " "	" "		Lieut Dunning returned from Base – Artillery Ho/s returned to their batteries direct from LUCHEUX – (S.E. Pte Pw GAMMON M.V.S. (reinforcement) joined unit – taken on strength	
" " "	28/1/19	9-35 a.m.	Marched off from LA FOLIE FARM via LUCHEUX – IVERGNY – REBREUVE tte to REBREUVE where billets occupied for night –	
" " "	1-2/1/19	8.30 a.m.	Marched from REBREUVE via FREVENT thence HEILLY via FIEFS to AVAIN where billets taken for the night – also Blisking of feelin Horses has been completed since leaving HUMBER R. CAMP – the horses have stood in the open – as Mange had recently been rife within the Division – it was decided to stop the use of rugs on the old Army principle that if the outbreak of their disease – all rugs should be withdrawn "No ill effects at all are noted – in fact the horses have stood the hard marching with not the slightest horses than to hot has been a force on both from bad wet conditions – from irregularity of watering	

2449 Wt. W14957/M90 750,000 1/16 J.B.C. & A. Forms/C.2118/12.

Army Form C. 2118.

WAR DIARY or **INTELLIGENCE SUMMARY**

1/1 R. Mobile Veterinary Section

There are 5 rugs issued and one for the Section horses only this month.

L.H.B.R.E.T. Rugs are only issued in larger cages in this unit.

During the month over three hundred sick horses have been dealt with by the unit - conditions were bad & the weather wastage - grooming was rendered difficult owing to water systems being frozen. The water cart had been a total indispensable. It is remarked that horses are allowed to become far too emaciated + debilitated before they reach the hands of the Veterinary Service, though it would appear that T. O. & Ve Units are also responsible in the matter. The bad state of the roads for marching - after the frost thaw - heavy traffic has been commented upon and the transport of this unit is insufficient. The Horse Ambulance is an unsuitable vehicle for first line transport. It is too long on the ground. The tyres are much too narrow - the vehicle itself is far heavier than would appear to be necessary - the universally on the unit of March + one would suggest that to small unit would listen owing into traffic if allowed to March independently by rail or rafter for destinations would especially the way to reach Birmingham. Also ?

R.M. Foster Capt. A.V.C.
Captain R.M.V.S.

Vol 21

SECRET.

WAR DIARY.

OF

1/1st (WR) Mobile Veterinary Section

FOR

March 1917.

WAR DIARY or INTELLIGENCE SUMMARY

Army Form C. 2118.

Place	Date	Hour	Summary of Events and Information	Remarks and references to Appendices
Lillers	1/3/17	8/3am	The Unit Moved off from REBREUVE via FREVENT/HERLIN LE SEC/ ST POL/ WARRANS - DANVIN where billets were taken up for the night - 9 P.O.T. was reached 2 p.m. Horses were off saddled, transport unhooked, hand rubbed - watered & fed - a halt of ½ her hour & a half - ANVIN was not reached until after 7 p.m. owing to congestion of the road in front by D.A.C.	
" "	2/3/17	10am	Unit moved off from ANVIN - marched via BERGUENEUSE - FONTAINE LES BALANS to FONTAINE LES HERMANS - where billets were taken for the night - During the march G.O.C. Division inspected the Unit & remarked that the animals looked well but the saddlery & harness were dirty - N.C.O's & men were paraded the same night & informed & steps are being taken to remedy this matter - there can be no doubt that since the Section again in January this year the want of discipline, accompanied with the standard of which previously existed in the Unit has been	15/30 of E.M.

CAPTAIN, A.V.C.
8/6. 1/1 W.R. MOBILE VETERINARY SECTION.

WAR DIARY or INTELLIGENCE SUMMARY

Army Form C. 2118.

Place	Date	Hour	Summary of Events and Information	Remarks and references to Appendices
Lillers	2/3/17	7 p.m.	Most noticeable — up to October last year — there was a totally standard. The men here to become criminals but they have become awfully slack.	
	3/3/17		Unit moved from Fontaine les Hermans via Westrehem — LIGNY-LES-AIRE — RELY — ST HILAIRE — LILLERS — BUSNES — Roberg — ST ALONNE where billets were taken up for the night — Had rather a bad inclement night — at BUSNES —	
	4/3/17		At CALONNE — O.C. Visited LESTREM interviewed A.D.V.S. there — Subsequently went to LA GORGUE — Ewel Major Ascot A.D.V.S. 56 Div — Captain Anthony O.C. M.V.S. —	
	5/3/17		Took Regl Mates — Pte Batty (today) to section lines at LA GORGUE	
	6/3/17		Marched section from Calonne to LA GORGUE — took over picketines Billets etc, vacated by M.V.S. 56th Division. —	
	8-3-17		Parade for advance of Pay — 2 p.m. at the office.	
	9-3-17		32 Horses & Mules (12 cases of Mange & 1 case of Ulceratic Cellulitis included) railed to Base to-day from LA GORGUE Station i/c 2nd Cpl Knighton & 4 Men.	

Army Form C. 2118.

WAR DIARY
or
INTELLIGENCE SUMMARY
(Erase heading not required.)

Place	Date	Hour	Summary of Events and Information	Remarks and references to Appendices
In the Field	9-3-17		A.D.V.S. visited and inspected Sections & Evacuation Cars & Billets. Float made on journey to Station.	
" "	9-3-17		No. TT 03156 Pte. Furner W.H. A.V.C. admitted 1/(NR) Field Ambulance.	
" "	9-3-17		No. TT 03203 Pte. S. Fawley A.V.C. was awarded 6 extras guards for absence off Post at mid-day stable guard.	
" "	10-3-17		No. 14495 Pte. Hainsworth (6 West Yorks Regt.) returned to his Unit.	
" "	10-3-17		SE. 3983 Pte. Todd G. A.V.C. arrived as a reinforcement from No.1 Veterinary Hospital, LACHAPELLE - AUX - POTS. and is taken on the Strength of the Section from 10-3-17.	
" "	10-3-17		Float made two journeys to line of 2 + 5 (NR) Bde R.F.A. and floats horse to M.V.S.	
" "	11-3-17		Horse detected salivating copiously - picked out - examined over-grown Molars. Zerion, Lips Gums and tongue probably Traumatic Suspected ADVS informed by wire. Stomatitis	
" "	12-3-17		A.D.V.S. visited lines and inspected horse particularly Stomatitis Case.	

O.C. 1/1 W.R. MOBILE VETERINARY SECTION.
CAPTAIN, A.V.C.
E.V. Foster

WAR DIARY or INTELLIGENCE SUMMARY

Army Form C. 2118.

Place	Date	Hour	Summary of Events and Information	Remarks and references to Appendices
In the field	12-3-17		Horse No 4020 Black Gelding destroyed suffering from Parophymia. Horse No 4041 Chesnut Gelding destroyed suffering from Parophymia. Carcases handed over to M. JULES DELOS, 42 Rue du Lille, Estaires. (Horse Boutcher).	
" "	12-3-17			
" "	13-3-17		31 Horses embarked at Estaires to-day for No 23 Veterinary Hospital ST OMER i/c Sgt. Cpl. G. Pickering, Pte Fawley, Farrier.	
" "	13-3-17		32 Horses 5 mules (4 cases of Mange, 12 cases of Ulcerative Cellulitis included) railed to Bern to-day from LA GORGUE Station i/c Corporal Cook, Pte Todd, Haines, Hallworth and Burfield.	
" "	13-3-17		A.D.V.S. visits and inspects Section.	
" "	13-3-17		Horse No 4085 Tested with mallein 12-3-17. No reaction. This Animal showed Buccal lesions suspicious of Stomatitis. 13-3-17 mid-day got down unable to rise — Destroyed for Asthenia. In Field I Pony Mare, Pte Fennell - Snyder - Today him to Gunner returned from the Barn to-day. The Cpl. being the culprit struck to me handling over the following casualties occurred. Horse with fractured leg — 3 also being so.	C.G. 4/1 W.R. MOBILE VETERINARY SECTION. CAPTAIN, A.V.C. A.V.C.
" "	14-3-17			

WAR DIARY or INTELLIGENCE SUMMARY

Army Form C. 2118.

Place	Date	Hour	Summary of Events and Information	Remarks and references to Appendices
In the Field	14-3-17		Horse No. 4027 Bay gelding H.D. suffering from Stomatitis destroyed by order of 1 D.V.S. First Army	
" "	14-3-17		O.C. M.V.S. attended inspection of surplus horses of Division by D.D.R. First Army	
" "	14-3-17		T.T. 03199 Pte. # Attwimon A.V.C. admitted 1/(wa) Field Ambulance	
" "	16-3-17		T.T. 03199 Pte. # Attwimon A.V.C. discharged to duty from 1/(wa) Field Amb. 27 Horses 23 Mules railed to Base to-day from La Gorgue Station 1/C Corporal Brayley & 5 men. All mange cases. O.C. D.V.S. visited and inspected herds for evacuation.	
" "	17-3-17		Corporal G. Cooke, Pte Burfield-Hallworth-Haines and Todd returned from Base to-day.	
" "	17-3-17		O.C. & Sergt Stevening-Lance & Pte. Batty proceeded to Calonne-Sur-la-Lys and collected horse ex-bay 5/6 Divisional Train from Madam PATOV LA ROUX	
" "	17-3-17		O.C. visited Field Cashier at Hinges	

O. C. 1/1 W.R. MOBILE VETERINARY SECTION.
CAPTAIN, A.V.C.

WAR DIARY
or
INTELLIGENCE SUMMARY

Army Form C. 2118.

Place	Date	Hour	Summary of Events and Information	Remarks and references to Appendices
In the Field	17-3-17		Conv. No. 4628 (Book IX) Bay Gild to D suffering from Punctured Wound O. took four outbreaks at Abbatoir at Estaires By Sergt yabrants Carcas sold to Butcher.	
" "	17-3-17		Corporal G. Cooke AVC reported occurrences of fire in one truck. No damage to Animals - men - or truck only some forage burnt.	
" "	18-3-17		No. T.T. 03203 Pte. S. Fawley AVC admitted / (AVR) Field Ambulance.	
" "	19-3-17		The Other Ranks are temporarily attached to this Unit to as Conducting Party. Sick horses to the Base. No. 935250 Bombdr Humphries Q. No. 2830 Gunner Thurlow A. No. 1802 Gunner Banks G.p. No. 83566 Driver Levitt W. No. 47621 Gunner Mart. T. 1309 Gunner Grotehildt. No. 1446 Gunner Weymouth R. No. 47204 Driver Boheise call of 262 Bde Army Field Artillery. D.A.D.M.S. visited and inspected lines. D.A.Q.M.G visited and inspected lines.	
" "	20-3-17		34 horses embarked at Estaires to-day for No. 2.3 Veterinary Hospitals ST-OMER / c Bpt. Cooke Bombdn. Humphries and Driv Levitts.	

WAR DIARY
or
INTELLIGENCE SUMMARY

Army Form C. 2118.

Place	Date	Hour	Summary of Events and Information	Remarks and references to Appendices
X 15 Aire	26-3-17		31 Horses (15 cases of Mange included) railed to Base to-day from the lines in States i/c S/Sgt. Knighton & Gunner Thorburg-Barker & Waymouth.	
"	27-3-17		O.C. A.V.S. visited and inspected horses for evacuation.	
"	27-3-17		O.C. visited Rolncy and collected milk here from M. Louis Marle Rue de la Brasserie Rolncy. L/S-Cpl 64 M.G. Coy.	
"	27-3-17		No TT 03203 Pte Fawley S. was discharged to duty from 1/(WR) Field Ambulance.	
"	20-3-17		No TT 03156 Pte Turner W.H. was admitted to 1/2 London CCS at Merville	
"	27-3-17		SE 13364 S/Smith. Belsham AVC arrived as a reinforcement from No 8 Veterinary Hospital and is taken on strength ps of this Unit from to-day.	
"	27-3-17		No TT 03200 S/Smith Pratt AVC is permitted to revert to the rank of Private at his own request with pay effect from to-day.	

O.C. 1/1 W.R. MOBILE VETERINARY SECTION.
CAPTAIN, A.V.C.

WAR DIARY or INTELLIGENCE SUMMARY

Army Form C. 2118.

Place	Date	Hour	Summary of Events and Information	Remarks and references to Appendices
In the Field	22.3.17		No: TT 03200 Pte W.H. Pratt a/c. entrained at Ju Jugu State for No 2 Veterinary Hospital. Have now gone to War Establishment.	
" "	22.3.17		Driver J. Cahill a/sc. admitted 1/(WR) Field Ambulance	
" "	21.3.17		Corporal Bradley and Pooli returned from Base to-day	
" "	21.3.17		Corporal Y. Cooke & Pooli returned from Base to-day. Cpl. Cooke reported that one horse died on way to Base	
" "	23.3.17		29 Horses 12 Mules railed to Base to-day from Ju Jugu 8 Others i/c Pte Cpl Dunning & 5 men. (36 cases of mange and 5 Remount Cases included.)	
" "	23.3.17		One of the above horses attached with colic before departure from Ju Jugu - detrained and brought to Section for treatment. Letter sent - to O.C. Referring Hospital	
" "	25.3.17		Case No: 4223 (Book IX) Bay mare # D. Stuffing from above - reveals P.M. revealed Congestion of the lungs & try drops pericardi	

O.G. 1/1 W.R. MOBILE VETERINARY SECTION.
CAPTAIN, A.V.C.

WAR DIARY
or
INTELLIGENCE SUMMARY

Army Form C. 2118.

Place	Date	Hour	Summary of Events and Information	Remarks and references to Appendices
Kut [Kutunia?]	26-3-17		No TT.03173 Pte. E. Batt A.V.C admitted 1/(WR) Field Ambulance	
"	26-3-17		Float made journey to Lasagne and Fronts is CRE's charges, thro' Mane.	
"	26-3-17		D.A.D.m.S. visited and inspected lines.	
"	26-3-17		Came No 4268 (Book IV) B his [held?] duck showing Colicky [symptoms]. P.m. revealed congestion of lungs. Extreme emaciation. [Being?] was [withdrawn?].	
"	27-3-17		10 Horses embarked at Estatis [Estatio?] to-day for No 2 & 3 Veterinary hospitals. St Anne 1/c Cpl C Bradley. Float made journey to Wharf	
"	27-3-17		Float made journey to Intrim and Pontoon Park Sick Home to Section from No 1 Pontoon Park R.E.	
"	27-3-17		1 Remount drawn from No 1 Coy 4/9 (WR) Divn Train.	
"	28-3-17		Float sent to No 1 Coy 4/9 (WR) Divn Train for repair. Water-Cart to No 1 Coy 4/9 (WR) Divn Train for repair.	

O.C. 1/1 W.R. MOBILE VETERINARY SECTION.
CAPTAIN, A.V.C.

WAR DIARY
or
INTELLIGENCE SUMMARY

Army Form C. 2118.

Place	Date	Hour	Summary of Events and Information	Remarks and references to Appendices
In the Field	28-3-17		Cpl. Dunning & 5 men returned from Base to-day. L/Cpl. Bradley returned from St. Omer to-day.	
" "	28-3-17		Bay Geld # D collected from Colonne arrivé to No 1 Coy 49 (Dur) Div. Train	
" "	29-3-17		No. T4/24985 Driver P. Glew asks attached to this Unit permitted to return to his Company at his own request.	
" "	29-3-17 10-20 am		Conv. No. 4284 (Book IV) 1 colt with Mallein 28-3-17. No reaction O/M put on morning Stables — went away unable to find destroyed	
" "	29-3-17		Conv. No. 4237 (Book IV) Bay Mare 16. suffering from Punctured N. Hock Joint destroyer. by Sergt. Evening farrier Carcass sold to Butcher.	
" "	30-3-17		7 horses returned to Base to-day from tow gauge Station L/Cpl. L. Pickering AVC. 5 cans of mange oil 2 cans of Mercuric Celluloid in stock.	

O.C. 1/1 W.R. MOBILE VETERINARY SECTION

WAR DIARY or INTELLIGENCE SUMMARY

Army Form C. 2118.

Place	Date	Hour	Summary of Events and Information	Remarks and references to Appendices
L.U.Lake	30.3.17		Canoe No 4124 (Book IV) Black Mare H.D. suffering from Submarine Abscess and Debility destroyed by Sergt Hemming. Cancer notes to Bulletin.	
" "	30.3.17		Canoe No. 4280 (Book IV) Bay Geld H.D. suffering from Navicular of Exuent destroyed by Sergt Hemming Palin. Cancer notes to Bulletin.	
" "	30.3.17		No T4/249613 Driver Henfall F. A.S.C. reported for duty and is attached for rations - duty and discipline with your remainders. Three hundred & twenty nine animals have passed through the sections during the month. The health of the personnel has been good with the exception of a few men who have suffered from frostbite inflicted wounds - an almost unavoidable circumstance. The weather has been cold rue & though the surroundings are good, the surrounding's are very muddy. A destemper hospital erected & the lines have been cleared off which had been allowed to accumulate before the time took over from the outgoing one.	[signature] Captain, A.V.C. O.C. G./1/1 W.R. Mobile Veterinary Section.

Vol 22

SECRET.

WAR DIARY.

OF

49th (West) Div¹ Mobile Vety Section

FOR

April 1917.

Army Form C. 2118.

WAR DIARY
or
INTELLIGENCE SUMMARY.

(Erase heading not required.)

Place	Date	Hour	Summary of Events and Information	Remarks and references to Appendices
In the Field	2-4-17	8.45am	Parade for Rifle inspection by the O.C.	
" "	1-4-17		Float returned to Section from No 1 Coy 49 (WR) Division	
" "	2-4-17		Float made journey to Thorentes and floated mule horse to Section Lines	
" "	3-4-17		12 Horse 2 Mules embarked at Estaires to-day for No 23 Veterinary Hospital St Omer. 1c/Cpl Knighton & Pte & Sammer	
" "	4-4-17		No T.T 03.17 G Pte & Haines AVC admitted 1/(WR) Field Ambulance	
" "	6-4-17		6 Horse (all mange cases) railed to Base to-day from 2.A. Congue Station	
" "			1/c Pte L/Cpl Dunning	
" "	8-4-17	11am	Church Parade. All Ranks C of E paraded under the O.C. and proceeded to attend Service at La Congue. All Ranks R.C. paraded under Sergt Herringham and proceeded to Service at La Congue Church 9-15am.	
" "			4 Horse 3 Mules embarked at Estaires for Base to-day 1/c Cpl Knighton and 1 man	
" "	10-4-17			
" "	11-4-17		1/c L/Cpl Knighton and 1 man returned from Base to-day	
" "	16-4-17		Parade for Advance of Pay at the Office 2 pm	

Army Form C. 2118.

WAR DIARY
or
INTELLIGENCE SUMMARY.
(Erase heading not required.)

Instructions regarding War Diaries and Intelligence Summaries are contained in F. S. Regs., Part II. and the Staff Manual respectively. Title pages will be prepared in manuscript.

Place	Date	Hour	Summary of Events and Information	Remarks and references to Appendices
In the Field	11-4-17	5 pm	Party under Sergt. Theveningham assisted R.F.A. drivers to get G.S. Wagon out of ditch at Western edge of Estaires.	
" "	12-4-17		S.E. 1665 Pte French D. AVC., S.E. 21605 Pte Lawrence oh. AVC arrived as a reinforcement from No 6 Veterinary Hospital Rouen and are taken on the strength of this Unit from 12-4-17.	
" "	2/4-4-17		No T.T. 03/70 Pte. J. Harris AVC. evacuated to 1/2 London C.C.S. Struck off the strength of this Unit from 4-4-17.	
" "	14-4-17		T.T. 03/87 Sergt. G.G. Yates AVC admitted 1/(WR) Field Ambulance suffering from Tonsilitis	
" "	15-4-17		Unit paraded mounted full strength with transport 9-45 am. Inspected by A.D.V.S. 49(WR)Division and immediately afterwards by G.O.C. 49(WR)DIVISION. Parade on La Gorgue - Estaires Road. G.O.C. expressed satisfaction as result of Inspection and instructed O.C. to convey to all Ranks his appreciation of the very smart way in which the Unit turned out with regard to Personnel-Horses and Equipment. A.D.V.S. subsequently addressed the Parade	O.C. 1/1 W.R. MOBILE VETERINARY SECTION, CAPTAIN, A.V.C.

Army Form C. 2118.

WAR DIARY
or
INTELLIGENCE SUMMARY.
(Erase heading not required.)

Instructions regarding War Diaries and Intelligence Summaries are contained in F.S. Regs., Part II. and the Staff Manual respectively. Title pages will be prepared in manuscript.

Place	Date	Hour	Summary of Events and Information	Remarks and references to Appendices
In the Field	15-4-17		Lines visited by Portuguese Officers accompanied by Staff Major Twist. Army Information as to routine running of a British M.V.S. given to Portuguese Officers.	
" "	15-4-17		No. T.T. 03187 Sergt-G.E.H. Yates A.V.C. evacuated to No. 57 C.C.S. Struck off the strength of this Unit from 15-4-17.	
" "	16-4-17		F.O.M. visited Section and examined Horse Ambulance. Condemned by F.O.M. and authority given to Report for one to replace one completely broken down	
" "	18-4-17		22 horses embarked at Estairres to-day for 23 Veterinary Hospital. St Omer i/c Lce Cpl G. Pickering A.V.C and 2 mend	
" "	19-4-17		No. T.T. 03161 Corporal G. Bradley A.V.C. admitted (our) Field Ambulance	
" "	20-4-17		4 Horses (2 cases of Mange & 2 cases of pis included) railed to Base to-day from La bergue Station i/c Lce Cpl P. Dunning act	
" "	20-4-17		Horse No. 4346 (Book X) destroyed suffering from Debility-pies and Catarrh	
" "	20-4-17		Horse No. 4356 and 4365 (Book X) destroyed. P.M exam showed Gangrenous Pneumonia and in case of 4356 Septic Pleurisy	

CAPTAIN, A.V.C.
O.C. 1/1 W.R. MOBILE VETERINARY SECTION.

WAR DIARY
or
INTELLIGENCE SUMMARY.
(Erase heading not required.)

Army Form C. 2118.

Place	Date	Hour	Summary of Events and Information	Remarks and references to Appendices
In the Field	21-4-17		No T.T.03161 Corporal C. Bradley A.V.C. discharged to duty from 1/(W) Field Ambulance.	
" "	22-4-17		(Cover No. 4347 (Book X) 5 a.m. showed symptoms Colic. Died 7 a.m. P.M. recom Ruptured Stomach & Peritonitis.	
" "	23-4-17		No T.T.03227 Pte J. Burchfield A.V.C. awarded 5 days forfeiture of Pay 21-4-17 Offence Not wearing Gas Helmet Disobedience of Standing Orders	
" "	24-4-17		19 Horses 6 mules, embarked at La Gorgue for Base to-day 1/W.6.M Knights & 2 men.	
" "	25-4-17		Parade for Advances of Pay at the Office 2 p.m.	
" "	25-4-17		T.T.027 Sergt E.L. Relf A.V.C. having arrived as a reinforcement from No 2 Veterinary Hospital Havre is taken on the strength of this Unit with effect from 23-4-17.	G.G.1/1 W.R. MOBILE VETERINARY SECTION, CAPTAIN, A.V.C. [signature]
" "	26-4-17		New ft Horse Ambulance French Pattern drawn from Ordnance to-day.	
" "	28-4-17		The following men were awarded "Good Conduct Badges" in completing a term of "good conduct" at the date against their names. SE.1665 Pte French D. 7-12-16. S.E.3256 Pte Gammon R.W. 9-1-17. T.T.03232 Pte Banks J. 26-4-17	

WAR DIARY
or
INTELLIGENCE SUMMARY.
(Erase heading not required.)

Army Form C. 2118.

Place	Date	Hour	Summary of Events and Information	Remarks and references to Appendices
Rem. Katfield	27-4-17		7 Horses 1 Mule (7 cases of Mange and one case of Ulcerative cellulitis included) railed to Rouen to-day.	O.C. 1/1 W.R. Mobile Veterinary Section, Captain, A.V.C.
" "	28-4-17		O.C. took detail to Busnes and collected a horse from Ligny Station & the 69th & Pickering Coys. which was cast-dropped to the Section Lines by Ambulance. Animal L/F behind by 4 & 5 D.A.C. suffering from Septic Arthritis of Pedal Joint. Also examined a Mule L/F behind by the same Unit.	
" "	29-4-17		Pte. Atkinson A.V.C. conducted Ambulance to Busnes and collected Mule suffering from Double Pneumonia and brought to the Animal Sick Lines.	
" "	29-4-17		T.T. 03165 Pte. H. Farrer A.V.C. admitted to 1 (N.B.) Field Ambulance.	
" "	30-4-17		A.D.V.S. visited and inspected lines.	
" "	30-4-17		Canine No 4403 (Book 7) destroyed suffering from Septic Arthritis of Pedal Joint. Dog destroyed for French Civilian Refugees from Shell Shock. Two Horses	
" "	30-4-17		Transport ordered by A.D.V.S. turn in the 3d and over in the 2d for removal of Baggage and Officers Pennies	

Army Form C. 2118.

WAR DIARY
or
INTELLIGENCE SUMMARY.
(Erase heading not required.)

Place	Date	Hour	Summary of Events and Information	Remarks and references to Appendices
Rm Riddle	20.4.17		Some convoy in Ambulance from lines of 2nd London Heavy Batty R.G.A. to M.V.S. Party under Command of O.M. proceeded to lines Bhelen & gun D.A.C. and took over fifteen Animals per evacuation	
" "	30.4.17		Parade for full strength 8-45 a.m. During the month the Personnel have paraded at the Divisional Baths each week & have been bathed and had change of underclothing. A small butter has been borrowed & used during the month. This is absolutely necessary when forage has to be used as a food. Several mares belonging to Civilians have been given necessary Veterinary attention. One horse brought in by a civilian has been found to belong to the British Government and instructions have been received to Mallein the Animal & previous to issue. One dog has been successfully treated for Rupture.	
" "	28.4.17		Radius to Ulna La Bagher under Enemy Shell fire. Railhead has been changed to Morville. The Casualties death-with have diminished very considerably when compared with those of the previous four months. Roads have been constructed and ground made good by	

A.M. Foster
CAPTAIN, A.V.C.
O.C. 1/1 W.R. MOBILE VETERINARY SECTION.

Army Form C. 2118.

WAR DIARY
or
INTELLIGENCE SUMMARY.
(Erase heading not required.)

Instructions regarding War Diaries and Intelligence Summaries are contained in F. S. Regs., Part II. and the Staff Manual respectively. Title pages will be prepared in manuscript.

Place	Date	Hour	Summary of Events and Information	Remarks and references to Appendices
			rolling Whitewashing has also been carried out. A constant supply of Calcium Bi-Sulphide Solution has been available and has been issued to Units as required	B.M.H.
			A.M. Foster	
			Captain, A.V.C.	
			O.C. 1/1 W.R. MOBILE VETERINARY SECTION.	

WAR DIARY
or
INTELLIGENCE SUMMARY.
(Erase heading not required.)

Mob Vety Sec
Vol 23

Place	Date	Hour	Summary of Events and Information	Remarks and references to Appendices
In the field	1-5-17		First Blankets withdrawn and bundled and returned to Winter Clothing Dump	
" " "	1-5-17		F.S. Boots withdrawn and returned to Winter Clothing Dump	
" " "	1-5-17		16 Ponies embarked at La Gorgue for Base to-day. P/6 P/Lockwood and Pte Lawrence.	
" " "	2-5-17		No T.T. 03165 Pte Farrer H. A.V.C. evacuated to No 54 C.C.S. Strength 2-5-17	
" " "	2-5-17		O.D.V.O visited and inspected Animals for evacuation	
" " "	4-5-17		4 Horses 2 Mules (5 cases of Mange and two cases of Lice included) railed to Base to-day from La Gorgue station. In charge of Pte J Knighton.	
" " "	4-5-17		No T.T. 03227 Pte Burfield J. A.V.C. was this day awarded 7 days Field Punishment No 1 with loss of Pay for "Not complying with an order".	
" " "	7-5-17		No T.T. 03198 Pte Hollowarth T. A.V.C. proceeded on leave to England from La Gorgue from 8-5-17 to 18-5-17	

Army Form C. 2118.

WAR DIARY
or
INTELLIGENCE SUMMARY.
(Erase heading not required.)

Instructions regarding War Diaries and Intelligence Summaries are contained in F.S. Regs., Part II. and the Staff Manual respectively. Title pages will be prepared in manuscript.

Place	Date	Hour	Summary of Events and Information	Remarks and references to Appendices
Le Kreule	7-5-17		One Bell R. (Section Rider) destroyed suffering from Ventral Hernia	
" "	8-5-17		5 Horses embarked at Peseque for Base to-day. L/c Dunning A.V.C.	
" "	8-5-17		No. TT.03199 Pte. O'Hanion H.A.V.C admitted (N.Z) Field Ambulance	
" "	9-5-17		Parade for Change of Pay at the Office 3 pm	
" "	10-5-17		No. TT.05 Pte White. M.A. A.V.C. arrived as a reinforcement from No.2 Veterinary Hospital Havre and is taken on the strength of this Unit from 9-5-17.	
" "	10-5-17		A/Cpl Jones (Section) despatched to No. 1 Field Remount Section GONNEHEM i/c Corporal G. Cooke (War Establishment temporarily reduced)	
" "	10-5-17		L/Cpl Dunning G A.V.C. returned from Base to-day	
" "	10-5-17		No TT.03199 Pte O'Hanion A.V.C discharged to duty from (N.Z) Field Ambulance	
" "	12-5-17		No.TT.03193 Pte Clarkson G.T. A.V.C. admitted "(N.Z) Field Ambulance	
" "	13-5-17		No. 13113 Black Mare H.D. 16-2 Type Star underlip 13½ letters destroyed suffering from Traumatic Septic Arthritis off fore,	
" "	14-5-17		Rifle Inspection 8. a.m 5 am by the OC.	

Army Form C. 2118.

WAR DIARY
or
INTELLIGENCE SUMMARY.

(Erase heading not required.)

Instructions regarding War Diaries and Intelligence Summaries are contained in F. S. Regs., Part II. and the Staff Manual respectively. Title pages will be prepared in manuscript.

Place	Date	Hour	Summary of Events and Information	Remarks and references to Appendices
In Field	14-3-17		No T.T. 03199 Pte E.J. Clarkson A.V.C discharged to duty from Hostility Ambulance	
" "	15-5-17		No T.T. 02032 Pte Tennyct T.B. A.V.C is awarded Corpl Pay at 1/6 four/th	
			Rats (6" rudiens) with effect from 16-5-16.	
" "	15-3-17		21 Horses embarked at Le Hogue for Base to-day & to Cpl S.	
			Pickering A.V.C.	
" "	17-5-17		Inspection of Anti-Gas Appliances by the D.D.V.S.	
" "	21-5-17		No T.T. 03185 Pte HALLSWORTH T. A.V.C. returned from leave in England	
			Rifle Inspection by the O.C. 8.45 am	
" "	22-5-17		10 Horses all mange cases) railed to Rouen to-day from Le Gogue Siding	
			to Lieut Cpl. J. Dickering A.V.C. and Pte Burfield	
" "	23-5-17		Parade for attendance of Coy at the Office 5 pm.	
" "	23-5-17		No T.T. 03185 Pte Hallsworth T. A.V.C. has this day awarded forfeiture	
			of 5 days Pay and Corps for making an improper reply to an	
			N.C.O.	
" "	25-5-17		No T.T. 03198 Pte Hallworth T. A.V.C. admitted 1/(WR) Field Ambulance	
" "	23-5-17		Lu Cpl. J. Dunning and Pte Burfield returned from Base to-day.	

Army Form C. 2118.

WAR DIARY
or
INTELLIGENCE SUMMARY.

(Erase heading not required.)

Place	Date	Hour	Summary of Events and Information	Remarks and references to Appendices
In Field	27-5-17		No T.T. 03203 Pte S. Fawley A.V.C. detailed 1/(W.R.) Field Ambulance	
" "	27-5-17		No SE.3256 Pte R.W. Gammon A.V.C. is appointed Section Barker	
			vice No TT 03203 Pte S. Fawley A.V.C. with effect from 1-5-17.	
" "	28-5-17		T.T.03163 A/Cpl D. Dunning A.V.C. admitted 1/(W.R) Field Ambulance	
" "	28-5-17		No T.T.03198 Pte F. Hallward A.V.C. evacuated to No. 54 C.C.S	
			Strength 28-5-17.	
			Strength of Animals.	
" "	29-5-17		13 Horses 2 Mules (3 Cases of Mange and 1 Remount - 1 un-inoculated)	
			embarked at Le Havre for Base to-day, 1. Cpl G. Cooke	
			Cpl G. Cooke returned from Base to-day	
" "	30-5-17		No SE 1665 Pte French D. A.V.C was this day awarded 21 days	O.C. 1/1 W.R. MOBILE VETERINARY SECTION. CAPTAIN, A.V.C
" "	30-5-17		Field Punishment No 1 with loss of pay and forfeiture of good conduct	
			Badge, for the following offence 1. "Disobeying an order."	
			Section has behaved to the afternoon.	
" "	13-5-17		Sick horse placed in the afternoon	
" "	16-5-17		Sick horse placed in the afternoon on Breast line.	
" "	26-5-17		Lieut-Colonel O.W. Manor A.V.C. A.D.V.S. proceeded on leave to England	
" "	26-5-17		Captain A.N. Foster A.V.C. acting A.D.V.S. 49 (W.R) Division	

WAR DIARY
or
INTELLIGENCE SUMMARY.

Army Form C. 2118.

Place	Date	Hour	Summary of Events and Information	Remarks and references to Appendices
In the Field	31/5/17		During the latter part of the month Demonstrations have been given to the personnel of the whole Division in the use, carrying and application of the Anti Gas Horse Respirator. A shortage is being sent to G.H.Q. 4th C.R. Division on the subject, but the following remarks are made. It is simple in design & applications should appear to be practical. Animals do not resent it - nor do they shew distress when wearing it. Most of them sneeze rough & feel uneasy after the removal of the Respirator. Animals wearing Hessian Hoods will be more likely to be under control. The horse casualties have been very light in the Division during the month. Pieces on the estures weakly large for evacuation cases have been allotted 8 N.1.W. 1.S. & on the 29 inst., that unit sent down 14 cases. Horses belonging to French civilians have been given veterinary attention.	
	31-5-17			

A.M.Porter
CAPTAIN, A.V.C.
O. C. 1/1 W. R. MOBILE VETERINARY SECTION.

Vol 24

SECRET.

WAR DIARY.

OF

4pt (W.R.) Mob Vet Sect

FOR

June 1917.

Army Form C. 2118.

WAR DIARY
or
INTELLIGENCE SUMMARY.
(Erase heading not required.)

Instructions regarding War Diaries and Intelligence Summaries are contained in F. S. Regs., Part II. and the Staff Manual respectively. Title pages will be prepared in manuscript.

Place	Date	Hour	Summary of Events and Information	Remarks and references to Appendices
In the Field	1-6-17		No. T.T 03163 L/Cpl J Dunning A.V.C discharged to duty from X Corps Rest Station	
" "	1-6-17		No. T.T 03176 Pte b/Cpl J Knighton A.V.C admitted 1/(W.R) Field Ambulance.	
" "	2-6-17		Six cases of mange failed to Base to-day from La Gorgue Station i/c Pte Cocker	
" "	2-6-17		No. T.T 03191 Sergt. Alf Hemingham A.V.C. proceeded on leave to England. Leave granted from 3-6-17 to 13-6-17.	
" "	2-6-17		T.T 03176 Pte b/Cpl J Knighton and R/10 T.T 03203 Pte S Fawley A.V.C evacuated to No. 54 CCS. Struck off strength of this Unit 2-6-17	Major [signature] A.V.C. CAPTAIN, MOBILE VETERINARY SECTION. O.C. 1/1 W.R.
" "	4-6-17	8.45am	Parade for Rifle Inspection by the O.C.	
" "	5-6-17		16 Horses (Foal included) mules embarked at La Gorgue for Base to-day i/c b/Cpl Carter	
" "	5-6-17		8 horses (Mange Cases) railed to Base to-day from La Gorgue Station i/c Cpl Bradley	
" "	5-6-17		No. SE 20663 Pte b/H Kaye A.V.C arrived as a reinforcement from No 4 Veterinary Hospital. Taken on strength of this Unit 5-6-17	
25-5-17 to 12-6-17			Captain D.N Foster A.V.C acting A.D.V.S 49th (W.R) Division during the absence of Lieut-Colonel Moron A.V.C on leave in England.	
In the Field	6-6-17		Cpl L Cooke returned from Base to-day	
" "	6-6-17		Parade for Advance of Pay at the Orderly Room 5 p.m.	

WAR DIARY
or
INTELLIGENCE SUMMARY.

Army Form C. 2118.

Place	Date	Hour	Summary of Events and Information	Remarks and references to Appendices
In the Field	7-6-17		No. TT 03163 Lce Cpl. T. Dunning A.V.C. proceeded on leave to England. Leave granted from 8-6-17 to 18-6-17.	
" "	7-6-17		Corporal Bradley returned from Base to-day.	
" "	10-6-17		No. SE 12852 Pte A.J. Every A.V.C. arrived as a reinforcement from No 3 Veterinary Hospital. Taken on the strength of this Unit from 10-6-17	
" "	11-6-17	8.45am	Parade for Rifle Inspection by the O.C.	
" "	12-6-17		6 Animals embarked at La Gorgue to-day for Base i/c Cpl Cooke. Also 7 mules and 1 Horse of No 57 M.V.S. 5 Mange cases of M.V.S. 1st Cavalry Division and 2 Horses of No 42 M.V.S. 32nd Division.	
" "	12-6-17		Lieut-Colonel A.W. Moran A.V.C. returned from leave in England. Captain A.N. Foster A.V.C. handed over A/ADVS 13-6-17.	
13-6-17 to 24-6-17			Captain A.N. Foster A.V.C. took over Veterinary Charge of the following Units viz: Captain D. Neil A.V.C. on leave in England. A.Q. 49 (WR) DIV. R.E. 49 (WR) Signal Coy R.E. 57th Field Coy R.E. 8 Y Cable Section R.E. C/332 Batty Army F.A. 1/1 (WR) Field Ambulance 3 Riding Horse Remounts Taken on strength of Section	
In the Field	13-6-17			

Major
C.W. Foster
D.C. 1/1 W.R. Mobile Veterinary Section.

WAR DIARY
or
INTELLIGENCE SUMMARY.
(Erase heading not required.)

Army Form C. 2118.

Place	Date	Hour	Summary of Events and Information	Remarks and references to Appendices
In the Field	13-6-17		No. S.E. 14184 Pte E.A.L. Jackson A.V.C. arrived as a reinforcement from No 22 Veterinary Hospital Abbeville. Taken on strength of this Unit 13-6-17.	
" "	14-6-17		No. T.T. 08171 Sergt. A.G. Heveringham A.V.C returned from leave in England. 8 horses (mange cases) railed to Base 15-day from Lagnicourt Station 1/c 2nd Cpl. G. Pickering A.V.C.	
" "	15-6-17		O.C. accompanied by Sergt. S.T. Relf A.V.C. visited Farm of M. DUBRULE Estaires and removed Foetal membranes from a Cow	
" "	16-6-17		No. S.E. 1665 Pte D. French A.V.C. returned to duty from A.P.M.	
" "	18-6-17	8.45am	Parade for Rifle Inspection by the O.C.	
" "	19-6-17		5 horses (1 card of Ulceratic Lymphatitis included) embarked at La Longue for Base 15-day 1/c L/Cpl Bradley 8 horses (all mange cases) railed to Base 15-day from La Longue Station 1/c Pte Hodgkin A.V.C.	
" "	20-6-17		No. T.T. 03163 2nd Cpl T. Denning A.V.C. returned from leave in England Parade for Advance of Pay at Orderly Room 8.45am.	
" "	21-6-17		No. T.T.03162 L/Cpl. G. Cooke A.V.C. temporarily attached H.Q. 146 Inf. Bde via Sergt. H. Redfearn A.V.C on leave at England	

C.W. Foster Major
O.C. No. 14 W.R. MOBILE VETERINARY SECTION.

Army Form C. 2118.

WAR DIARY
or
INTELLIGENCE SUMMARY.
(Erase heading not required.)

Place	Date	Hour	Summary of Events and Information	Remarks and references to Appendices
In the Field	21-6-17		Pte Hodgkins returned from Base to-day	
" "	22-6-17		Lieut-Colonel Cochrane AVC ADVS XI Corps accompanied by ADVS HQ (WR) Division visited Section and witnessed a demonstration of the Horse Eye Respirator Anti-Gas Horse Respirator.	
" "	22-6-17	8 pm	Horse Ambulance in charge of Sergt-Hemingham AVC proceeded to XI Corps Show Ground and Mule Block muck field to Section Lines.	
" "	23-6-17		Transport Horses and Drivers lent on loan to 5"/Y of L Regt at Vieille Chapelle. Returned at Lines of 5"/Y of L Regt 9.15 am returned to Section 4-30 pm	
" "	23-6-17		Float made journey to Lines of A/246 Batty RFA and Mule Sub lines to Sytin lines.	
" "	24-6-17		OC accompanied by Sergt-Hemingham visited the farm of M ERAISNEL LEQUIEN. N° 7 Clyde Road RIEZ BAILLEUL and examined a cow suffering from 8 or 9 wounds caused by an exploding missle. Report forwarded to Claims Officer 49(WR) Division	
" "	25-6-17		N° TT. 03162 Cpl L Cotter AVC granted leave to England 2-6-6-17 to 6-7-17.	

Major

O.C. 1/1 W.R. MOBILE VETERINARY SECTION.
CAPTAIN. A.V.C.

Army Form C. 2118.

WAR DIARY
or
INTELLIGENCE SUMMARY.
(Erase heading not required.)

Place	Date	Hour	Summary of Events and Information	Remarks and references to Appendices
In the field	25-6-17		No. T4/249655 Driver J. Cahill A.S.C. proceeded on leave to England from 26-6-17 to 6-7-17	
" "	25-6-17		No. T.T. 83161 Cpl. Bradley A.V.C. temporarily attached H.Q. 146 Infantry Brigade vice Cpl. Cooke on leave in England	
" "	25-6-17	9 pm	Lce. Cpl. Simpson 1st Batt. Notts and Derby Regt. reported to this Unit for inspection. Conv. No. 4527 Bay Mare & D handed over to this Unit by A.P.M. 13-6-17 issued to 1/4 K.O.Y.L.I. for duty 15-6-17 on authority H.Q. 49th (WR) Division. Report forwarded to H.Q. Division.	Meyer
" "	26-6-17	10 am	D.A.Q.M.G. Division visited Section and instructed Lce. Cpl. Simpson to proceed to H.Q. 148 Infantry Bde. from there Lce. Cpl. Simpson was sent to the lines of the 1/4 K.O.Y.L.I. at Vieille Chapelle and there picked out Conv. No. 4527 from a line of horses.	M. Feber
" "		2:30 p	Returned to Section in the afternoon remained that night with this Section and on 27-6-17 returned to his Unit with the horse.	
" "	26-6-17		8 Horses (5 cans of Mange included) embarked at Le Gorgue for Rouen to-day I/C Lce. Cpl. T. Dunning A.V.C.	

WAR DIARY
INTELLIGENCE SUMMARY

Army Form C. 2118.

Place	Date	Hour	Summary of Events and Information	Remarks and references to Appendices
In the Field	26.6.17		No. T.T. 03032 Pte Tennet T.B. A.V.C. to awarded a "Good Conduct Badge" with effect from 9-6-17 on completion of a period of Good Conduct.	
" "	26.6.17		No. T.T. 03203 Pte S. Fawley A.V.C. discharged to duty from No. 54 C.C.S. No. T.T. 03193 Pte G. F. Clarkson A.V.C. is appointed Unpaid acting Lance-Corporal with effect from 26-6-17.	
" "	27.6.17		L/Cpl S. Dunning A.V.C. returned from Base to-day.	
" "	27.6.17		Sergt. Heavingham A.V.C. visited & examined in Estaires and examined horse injured by aeroplane bomb explosion. Arterial Haemorrhage and debrided wounds. Subsequently examined by Mr. Tetanus Antitoxin and Strychnine administered.	
" "	27.6.17		O.C. accompanied by Sergt. Heavingham visited farm at RIEZ BAILLEUL, treated wounds and administered dose of Tetanus Antitoxin to cow suffering from wounds caused by and exploding mine.	
" "	28.6.17		7 Horses (Mange Cases) railed to Base to-day from La Gorgue Station i/c Pte Laurence	

O.C. No. 14 W.R. Mobile Veterinary Section.

Army Form C. 2118.

WAR DIARY
or
INTELLIGENCE SUMMARY.
(Erase heading not required.)

Place	Date	Hour	Summary of Events and Information	Remarks and references to Appendices
In Field	30-6-17		No. T.T. 03193 Dvr - Corporal G.F. Clarkson A.V.C. proceeded on leave to England. Leave granted from 1-7-17 to 11-7-17.	
" "	30-6-17		No. T.T. 03203 Pte S. Fawley A.V.C proceeded on leave to England. Leave granted from 1-7-17 to 11-7-17.	
" "	30-6-17		O.C. accompanied by Sergt Beveningham AVC visited farm at RIEZ BAILLEUL and found wothed on a cow caused by an exploding missile.	

O.W. Foster MAJOR.
O.C. 1/1 W.R. MOBILE VETERINARY SECTION.

MOBILE VETERINARY SECTION
49th (W.R.) DIVISION
Date 30-6-17

Secret

War Diary Vol 25
of
Nec W.R. Bure Ver Sect
for
July 1917

WAR DIARY
or
INTELLIGENCE SUMMARY

Army Form C. 2118.

(Erase heading not required.)

Place	Date	Hour	Summary of Events and Information	Remarks and references to Appendices
Stirling Castle	1/6/17		Capt. & Colonel G. W. Mason A.V.C. A.D.V.S. appointed to 2nd N.Z. ANZAC Corps.	
" "	" "		Major A. H. FOSTER A.V.C. assumed duties of D.A.D.V.S. 2 N.Z. & 9 E.G.R. Division	
" "	" "		Major Westgate Mason A.V.C. visited Lines - all ranks & Section Paraded & addressed by Colonel Mason.	
" "	2-7-17		S.S. Lanka & Wagon transported Col. Mason's luggage from to Sarjeu to Boulland	
La Motte	2-7-17		Parade for R.V.C. Inspection by the O.C.	
" "	3-7-17		Pte. Lawrence returned from Base to-day.	
" "	3-7-17		10 Horses embarked at La Gorgue for Base to-day if Pte Burfield.	
" "	3-7-17		6 Horses (all Mange Cases) Railed to Base to-day from La Gorgue Station i/c Pte Ottaway	
" "	4-7-17		Parade for Advances of Pay at the Orderly Room 8.45am	
" "	4-7-17		Pte. Burfield returned from Base to-day.	
" "	4-7-17		Cpl. C. Bradley A.V.C. returned to his Unit from 146 Infantry Bde. Handed over to Sergt - Redfearn AVC 3-7-17	
" "	5-7-17		Pte. Ottaway AVC returned from Base to-day	

WAR DIARY
or
INTELLIGENCE SUMMARY.

Army Form C. 2118.

(Erase heading not required.)

O.C. 1/1 W.R. MOBILE VETERINARY SECTION.

Place	Date	Hour	Summary of Events and Information	Remarks and references to Appendices
In the Field	6/7/17		Corse No 4354 Black gld. destroyed suffering from Traumatic Arthritis N. Hock Joint.	
" "	6/7/17		6 Horses (bel Mange Cases) railed to Base to-day from La Gorgue Station 1/c Pte French A.V.C.	
" "	7/7/17		Float made its following journeys to-day and Carlist Sub Horses into the Station Cmb. (1) LAVENTIE (9 tons Furlong) (2) MERVILLE (66' D.A.C.) (3) NEUF BEQUIN (92 tons R.G.A.) Pte French A.V.C. returned from Base to-day.	
" "	8/7/17		Driver. J. Cahill A.S.C. returned from leave in England.	
" "	8/7/17		No T.T. 027 Sergt. REFF E. A.V.C. appointed to the rank of Staff Sergeant A.V.C. (Paid Acting Rank) with effect from 3-7-17. (Authority Army Veterinary Corps Total Corps Order No 66 of 3-7-17)	
" "	8/7/17		Cpl. G Crocker A.V.C. returned from leave in England	
" "	9/7/17		Parade for Rifle Instruction by the O.C. 8.45 am.	
" "	9/7/17		20 Horses Mules (Mange / Ulcerative Cellulitis and 1 case of Pneumonia including) embarked at La Gorgue for Base to-day 1/c Cpl. Bradley and Pte Evans	

Major
O.C. Vet.

WAR DIARY
or
INTELLIGENCE SUMMARY.
(Erase heading not required.)

Place	Date	Hour	Summary of Events and Information	Remarks and references to Appendices
In the field	10/7/17		A.D.V.S. & Corps visited Section and accompanied by Major Air Foster AVC proceeded to the place of embarkation and saw the animals embarked	
" "	16/7/17		12 Horses (all Mange cases) railed to Base 5 day premature Mange Station & L/Cpl J. Dunning AVC. 3 cases from No 1 M.V.S. & Cavalry Division included	
" "	9/7/17		No 562 Sergt M.A.WARD AVC invalided for duty from No 23 Veterinary Hospital St. OMER and to return on its strength 1 this Unit from 9-7-17.	
" "	10/7/17		20 Horses 5 mules (non Ulcerative Cellulitis and 1 case of Pneumonia included) embarked at La Gorgue for Base to-day. 1/c Corporal C Bradley and 1 man.	
" "	10/7/17		Following cases railed to Base to-day from La Gorgue Station 1/c L/Cpl J Dunning AVC. (9 cases of mange)	
" "	13/7/17		24 Horses 2 mules (12 cases of mange 2 Ulcerative Cellulitis included railed to Base to-day. 1/c L/Cpl J. Pickering & 3 men	

WAR DIARY or INTELLIGENCE SUMMARY

Army Form C. 2118.

Place	Date	Hour	Summary of Events and Information	Remarks and references to Appendices
La Motte	13-7-17		Captain D. Kerr A.V.C. took over the Command of the Mobile Veterinary Section vice Major A.N. Foster A.V.C. DADVS 49 (W.R) Division	O.C. 1/1 W.R. MOBILE VETERINARY SECTION. Handed over Capt
"	13-7-17		No T.T. 03462 Corporal G. Cooke A.V.C. admitted 1/(W.R) Field Ambulance	
"	14-7-17		Section vacated Billets at ESTAIRES. Marched 8 am. Entrained at LESTREM 10 pm. Detrained at DUKERQUE 7 pm the same evening and marched to COUDEKERQUE BRANCHE. Such Horses conveyed in Horse Ambulances from DUNKERQUE Station to Sick Lines	
"	15-7-17		Lt. Col. G. Pickering A.V.C. and 3 men returned from Base to day.	
"	16-7-17		D.A.D.V.S. 49 (W.R) Division visited Section and inspected Animals for evacuation.	
"	16-7-17		In accordance with instructions of D.A.D.V.S. the following men were despatched to XV Corps H.Q. with instructions to report to A.D.V.S. XV Corps. No T.T. 03199 Pte. H. Attewan A.V.C. T.T. 03227 Pte. J. Bushilot - SE 21605 Pte. A. Lawrence A.V.C. T.T. 027 Staff Sergt E.L. RELF A.V.C. proceeded on leave to England, leave granted from 18-7-17 to 28-7-17	

WAR DIARY
or
INTELLIGENCE SUMMARY.

Army Form C. 2118.

Place	Date	Hour	Summary of Events and Information	Remarks and references to Appendices
In the Field	15/7/17		No T.T. 03193 Pte (A/Cpl) G. F. Clarkson A.V.C. and Private Fawley A.V.C. returned from leave in England.	
"	16/7/17		Pte Attinson - Burfield - Lawrence returned from XV Corps Mobile Veterinary Detachment.	
"	18/7/17		5 Horses 2 Mules (2 cases of Pneumonia included) railed to Base to-day from DUNKERQUE Station c/o Pte E. B. MARVIN /4 No 7 2. B.	
"	19/7/17		Parade for Advance of Pay at 12 noon.	
"	19/7/17		Section vacated Bellevue at GOUDERKERQUE BRANCHE. Marched off 7-4-5am arrived new area 4-1pm. Took over the Stabling and Billets - also 19 Sick Animals from No 42 M.V.S. 32nd Division.	
"	22/7/17		No T.T. 03032 Pte E. Saylor No SE /21605 Pte A. Lawrence, SE. 12852 Pte A J Every dispatched to XV Corps M.V.D.	
"	23/7/17		SE. /3364 Shoeing Smith W. Belsham A.V.C. proceeded on leave to England Leave granted from 24-7-17 to 3-8-17.	
"	23/7/17		D.A.D.V.S. visited Section and inspected Animals for evacuation.	
"	24/7/17		3 9 Horses 3 Mules (18 cases of Mange and 2 Ulceration of Withers included) railed	

O.C. 1/1 W.W. Mobile Veterinary Section
A.V.C.

WAR DIARY
or
INTELLIGENCE SUMMARY.
(Erase heading not required.)

Army Form C. 2118.

Place	Date	Hour	Summary of Events and Information	Remarks and references to Appendices
In the Field	25-7-17		To Base to-day from ST. IDES BALDE Station 1/c 1/w Cpl J Dunning Pte Grammer - Jackson - Hodgkins and Kaye. Head-made three Journeys to Station.	
" "	26-7-17		N° T.T. 03161 Corporal C. Bradley A.V.C. Transferred to B. Echelon 4(WR) D.A.C. via N° T.T. 03223 Sergt. J. FARRAR A.V.C. Reverted to Rank of Private Authority D.A.D.V.S. 4 q (WR) Division letter N° 148.V.1 23-7-17. N° T.T. 03162 Corporal G. Cooper A.V.C. discharged to duty from N° 51 C.C.S. 26-7-17	3
" "	26-7-17		1/w Cpl. J Dunning A.V.C and party returned from Base to-day. N° T.T. 027 Staff/Sergeant E.L. Relf A.V.C. returned from leave in England	
" "	30-7-17		Parade for Advance of Pay 6 fand	
" "	30-7-17		D.A.D.V.S. visited Station and inspected animals for evacuation	
" "	31-7-17		21 Horses (13 cases of Mange and 2 Ulcerative Cellulitis included about Revment) Taken to Base to-day from ST. IDES BALDE Station 1/c Corporal G Cooper Pte French and Kaye.	

31-7-17

David Keir
CAPTAIN, A.V.C.
O.C. 1/1 W.R. MOBILE VETERINARY SECTION.

SECRET.

WAR DIARY.

OF

H.Q. XOR. Mot. Vet. Sec.

FOR

August 1917.

WAR DIARY or INTELLIGENCE SUMMARY

Army Form C. 2118.

Place	Date	Hour	Summary of Events and Information	Remarks and references to Appendices
In the Field	3-8-17		Section vacated Billets at COXYDE and marched to FERME PONSDITE and took over Billets and Horse lines from No 42. M.V.S. 32nd Division. 7 Sub Animals were taken over by the Section. Four Sub Animals were handed over to its in-coming Section at Coxyde.	
" "	5-8-17		No SE 13364 Shoeing Smith W. Belcham A.V.C. returned from leave in England.	
" "	6-8-17		A.D.V.S. XV Corps visited Section.	
" "	7-8-17		No T.T. 03162 Corporal G Cooke A.V.C. proceeded to H.Q. 147 Infantry Bde at Coxyde Bains to relieve Sergt D Greenwood A.V.C. proceeding on leave.	
" "	8-8-17		D.A.D.V.S. 49(WR) Division visited Section and inspected Animals for Evacuation.	
" "	11-8-17		Parade for Rifle Inspection 2-30 p.m. Inspection of Saddlery and Harness 2-45 p.m.	
" "	13-8-17		Parade for Advance of Pay at the Orderly Room 2-30 p.m.	

CAPTAIN A.V.C.
O.C. 1/1 W.R. MOBILE VETERINARY SECTION.

WAR DIARY
or
INTELLIGENCE SUMMARY.
(Erase heading not required.)

Army Form C. 2118.

Place	Date	Hour	Summary of Events and Information	Remarks and references to Appendices
In the Field	14/8/17		14 Horses (5 cases of Mange and 1 case of Ulcerative Cellulitis wound 1 Remount included) shifted to Base to-day from DUNKERQUE.	
" "	15.8.17		CANAL RAILHEAD. N° T.T. 03199 Pte H. Osterman A.V.C. was this day awarded 21 days Field Punishment N°1 for the following offence:- "Whilst on Active Service. Neglect of Duty."	
" "	16.8.17		N° T.T. 03174 Pte A. Kelly A.V.C. proceeded on leave to England. Leave granted from 17-8-17 to 27-8-17.	
" "	27.8.17		N° T.T. 03161 Corporal C. Bradley A.V.C. returned to this Section from B. Echelon H.Q. (WR) D.A.C.	
" "	23.8.17		N° T.T. 03162 Corporal G. Cooke A.V.C. returned to this Section from 147 Infantry Bde.	
" "	27.8.17		N° T.T. 03032 Pte T.B. Tennet A.V.C. has this day been awarded 7 days Field Punishment N°2 for the following offence:- "Whilst on Active Service. Absent from Stables 3.45 pm to 5 pm (1 hour 15 minutes)."	

WAR DIARY
or
INTELLIGENCE SUMMARY.

Army Form C. 2118.

Place	Date	Hour	Summary of Events and Information	Remarks and references to Appendices
En Rottefeld	28.8.17		7 Horse 1 Mule (2 cases of Suspected Mange and 2 cases of Ulceration Cellulitis included) railed to Base to-day from Dunkerque Canal Railhead i/c to Cpl Dunning and 1 man.	
" "	30.8.17		Cpl J Dunning A.V.C. and 1 man returned from Base to-day. During the month assistance has been rendered to the Civilian Farmers by the NCO's and men of the Section, in gathering their crops.	

David Kerr

CAPTAIN, A.V.C.
O.C. 1/1 W.R. MOBILE VETERINARY SECTION.

31-8-17

War Diary Vol 27
of
Mot (W.R.) Vet Sect
for
September 1917

Army Form C. 2118.

WAR DIARY
or
INTELLIGENCE SUMMARY.
(Erase heading not required.)

Instructions regarding War Diaries and Intelligence Summaries are contained in F. S. Regs., Part II. and the Staff Manual respectively. Title pages will be prepared in manuscript.

Place	Date	Hour	Summary of Events and Information	Remarks and references to Appendices
In the Field	4.9.17		No. T.T. 03161 Cpl. C. Bradley A.V.C detailed for duty with XV Corps M.V.D	
" " "	10.9.17		No. SE 1665 Pte. D. FRENCH A.V.C proceeded on leave to England. Leave granted from 11-9-17 to 21-9-17.	
" " "	11.9.17		21 Horses 1 Mule (1 6 cases of Mange and 1 case of Opthalmia included) railed to base to-day from DUNNERQUE CANAL Railhead i/c Cpl. Cooker Pte. Atkinson - Tennant	
" " "	12.9.17		No. 562 Sergt. M.A. WARD A.V.C detailed to proceed with Convalescents from 49 (W.R.) DIVISION, to the Shoeing ground of the II Anzac Corps.	Bracke[y] Captain A.V.C. O.C. 1/1 W.R. Mobile Veterinary Section.
" " "	14.9.17		No. SE Pte. W. HODGKINS A.V.C. proceeded on leave to England. Leave granted from 15-9-17 to 25-9-17.	
" " "	18.9.17		No. T.T. 03199 Pte. H. Atkinson A.V.C. proceeded on leave to England. Leave granted from 19-9-17 to 29-9-17.	
" " "	18.9.17		15 Horses 1 Mule railed to base to-day from DUNNERQUE Canal Railhead i/c 1/c Cpl. Pickering and 1 man.	

WAR DIARY
or
INTELLIGENCE SUMMARY
(Erase heading not required.)

Army Form C. 2118.

Place	Date	Hour	Summary of Events and Information	Remarks and references to Appendices
In the Field	20-9-17		No. ST. 1665 Pte. D. FRENCH. A.V.C. admitted No. 3 Canadian General Hospital suffering from a Sprained Right Ankle	
" "	22-9-17		6 Horses handed over to 15 XV Corps M.V.D. owing to this Unit being under orders to move.	
" "	22-9-17		Cpl. C. Bradley A.V.C. and 3 men returned to Section from XV Corps. M.V.D.	
" "	23-9-17	8:30 am	Section unit's Billets at LEFFRINCKOUCKE and marched to WORMHOUDT, arriving there 4:30 pm. Horses Lines and Billets were obtained for the night by the 2nd Cpl flasher, who had been detached on 22-9-17 to proceed with an Advance Billeting Party from the Division, under the orders of an Officer of the Machine Gun Coy.	Received 18/9 O.C. 1/1 W.R. Mobile Veterinary Section. Captain, A.V.C.
" "	24-9-17	7:30 am	Section marched to LEDERZEELE arriving there mid-day. Tents were obtained from the Area Commandant for accommodating the N.C.O's and men.	
" "	27-9-17		3 Horses H. Mules evacuated to No. 23 Veterinary Hospital	

WAR DIARY
or
INTELLIGENCE SUMMARY.

(Erase heading not required.)

Army Form C. 2118.

Place	Date	Hour	Summary of Events and Information	Remarks and references to Appendices
St. Omer			By road. Application was made through D.A.D.V.S. for the Motor Horse Ambulance from the Hospital to convey two floating cases. The Ambulance arrived at the Siding 7-45 a.m. when it was inspected by the D.A.D.V.S.	
In the Field	28.9.17 1-30p		Section marched from EDERZEELE, through ST. OMER to WIZERNES arriving there 8-30pm.	
"	29.9.17		N° SE 20663 Pte. G.H. RAYE A.V.C. admitted 1/2 (WR) Field Ambulance.	
"	29.9.17		Sergt. Hemmingham and 1 man proceeded to ROBECQ and collected 2 sick horses from the Farm of M. DUHOO-MARTOU left there by the 6th Royal Berks Regt.	
	30-9-17			

(Dawe K.)
CAPTAIN, A.V.C.
O.C. 1/1 W.R. MOBILE VETERINARY SECTION.

Vol 28

S E C R E T.

WAR DIARY

OF

I/1st A.A.R. Mobile Vet. Section

FOR

1st to 31st October 1917

5159
31.10.17

H.Q.
49 (WR) Division
through D.A.D.V.S.

Herewith War Diary of
1/1 (WR) Mobile Veterinary Section
for the month of October 1917.
Kindly acknowledge receipt
hereon.

[signature]
CAPTAIN, A.V.C.
O.C. 1/1 W.R. MOBILE VETERINARY SECTION.

WAR DIARY or INTELLIGENCE SUMMARY

Army Form C. 2118.

Place	Date	Hour	Summary of Events and Information	Remarks and references to Appendices
In the Field	1-10-17		No. SE/3256 Pte P.W. GAMMON A.V.C. proceeded on leave to England. Leave granted from 2-10-17 to 12-10-17.	
" " "	1-10-17		No. TH/249613 Driver F. Hoofall proceeded on leave to England. Leave granted from 2-10-17 to 1-11-17 (Time expired) for one month.	
" " "	2-10-17	7.30am	Section vacated Billets at WIZERNES and marched to HAZEBROUCK arriving 5pm.	CAPTAIN A.V.C. O.C. 1/1 W.R. MOBILE VETERINARY SECTION
" " "	3-10-17	12 noon	Section marched to WATOU arriving there 6pm.	
" " "	5-10-17		2 Anno. 2 Nubis evacuated to 1 Anzac Corps Veterinary C.C.S.	
" " "	5-10-17		No. 77.03.199 Pte H. Atkinson A.V.C returned from leave in England.	
" " "	5-10-17		No. 77.03032 Pte T.B. TENNET A.V.C. proceeded on leave to England. Leave granted from 6-10-17 to 16-10-17.	
" " "	6-10-17		Section vacated Billets at WATOU and proceeded to VLAMERTINGHE Area, there relieving No 1 New Zealand M.V.S. Twenty eight Sick and Wounded animals were taken over by this Section. No. 77.03.161 Corporal C. Bradley A.V.C. and No. 77.03.199 Pte H. Atkinson A.V.C. detailed for duty at an Advanced Veterinary Aid Post	

WAR DIARY or INTELLIGENCE SUMMARY

Army Form C. 2118.

Place	Date	Hour	Summary of Events and Information	Remarks and references to Appendices
Reninghelst	11-10-17		Situated at Mobile Gun Farm. Personnel withdrawn from the Advanced Post. Taken over by No. 1 N.Z. M.V.S.	
	11-10-17		Section vacated Billets in the Vlamertinghe area, relieved by No. 1 N.Z. M.V.S. and proceeded to WATOU. 30 Sick and Wounded animals handed over to No. 1 N.Z. M.V.S.	
	11-10-17		No. T.T. 03161 Cpl. C. BRADLEY, P.6. Attendant and Farriers attached for duty with ¥ Corps Veterinary C.C.S. at OUDERDOM.	
			No. S.E. 12852 Pte. A.J. EVERY A.V.C. attached to ¥ Corps Vet. C.C.S. from 13-10-17	
	13-10-17		No. S.E. 10516 Pte (A.6.R) L. PICKERING A.V.C. transferred to No. 22 Veterinary Hospital Abeville. Authority Officer i/c A.V.C. Base Reunto.	
	13-10-17		No. T.T. 63227 Pte. J. BURFIELD A.V.C. proceeded on leave to England. Leave granted from 14-10-17 to 24-10-17	
	15-10-17		No. SE. 26663 Pte R. to HAYS A.V.C. discharged to duty from Hospital. Taken on strength of Section from 15-10-17	
	15-10-17		No. SE. 3256 Pte P. W. GAMMON A.V.C. returned from leave in England.	

O.C. 11 W.R. MOBILE VETERINARY SECTION.
CAPTAIN, A.V.C.

WAR DIARY or INTELLIGENCE SUMMARY

Army Form C. 2118.

Place	Date	Hour	Summary of Events and Information	Remarks and references to Appendices
In the Field	17-10-17		No. T.T. 03203 Pte T. B. Tennet A.V.C. returned from leave in England.	
"	22-10-17		T.T. 03161 L/Cpl. C. Bradley A.V.C. and No. S.E. 12852 Pte A.J. Every A.V.C. returned at 4 Corps Veterinary C.C.S. by No. T.T. 03162 L/Cpl. G. Cooper A.V.C. and No. T.T. 03032 Pte F.B. Tennet A.V.C.	
" "	21-10-17		No. S.E. 20663 Pte G. H. Haye A.V.C. and No. T.T. 03203 Pte G. Sayles A.V.C. proceeded on leave to England. Leave granted from 22-10-17 to 1-11-17.	
" "	22-10-17		No. T.T. 08 Pte W.A. White A.V.C. admitted to 1/0 (WR) Field Ambulance 22-10-17 evacuated to No. 7 General Hospital 22-10-17 Etaples 22-10-17 sick with effect from 22-10-17.	
" "	23-10-17		No. S.E. 1665 Pte D. French A.V.C. arrived as a reinforcement from No. 2 Veterinary Hospital Havre and to taken on its strength of the section with effect from 18-10-17	
	26-11-17		No. T.T. 03162 P/A/L/Cpl. G. Cooper A.V.C. departed to No. 2 Veterinary Hospital Havre to undergo further training and examination for promotion to the rank of Sergeant A.V.C. Day of departure to a Field Unit.	Authority O/Maj. A.G./73/4/17 A.V.C. Base Records dated 21-10-17.

B.C.L.W.R. Mobile Veterinary Section.
Captain, A.V.C.

WAR DIARY
or
INTELLIGENCE SUMMARY.

Army Form C. 2118.

Place	Date	Hour	Summary of Events and Information	Remarks and references to Appendices
Ruthuil	25.10.17		No TT.03193 Pte (A/cpl) G. F. Clarkson A.V.C. promoted to the rank of A/P/A Corporal A.V.C. as a temporary measure.	
"	26.10.17		No TT.03193 Corporal G. F. Clarkson A.V.C. detailed for duty with y Corps Vety. C.C.S. and No TT.03162 Cpl. G. Cooke relieved.	
"	28.10.17		Section vacated Billets in the Winnizeele Area and marched to Stenvoorde Area. there pickets in the open and all Ranks under Canvas.	
"	30.10.17		Captain J. POLLARD A.V.C. assumed command of the 1/(WR) Mobile Veterinary Section vice Captain D. KEIR A.V.C. who relinquished Command on the 30th inst. During the month 196 Animals have been admitted to the Section and have been dealt with as follows. 78. Evacuated by Road to S.T. omer. 48. Evacuated to Rone through Corps Vety. C.C.S. 37. Handed over to No 1 N.Z. M.V.S. 30 Animals. Died & Destroyed 7. Discharged to Duty 19. 14 Animals remaining under treatment.	

[signature]
O.C. 1/1 W.R. MOBILE VETERINARY SECTION.

CAPTAIN, A.V.C.

Vol 29

SECRET.

WAR DIARY.

OF

1/1st W.R. Mob. Vet. Sect.

FOR

November 1917.

Army Form C. 2118.

WAR DIARY
or
INTELLIGENCE SUMMARY.
(Erase heading not required.)

Place	Date	Hour	Summary of Events and Information	Remarks and references to Appendices
In the Field	3-11-17		N° SE 20663 Pte C.H. Kaye A.V.C. returned from leave in England.	
" "	6-11-17		N° SE 20663 Pte C.H. Kaye A.V.C. awarded forfeiture of 5 days pay for the following offence. Whilst on Active Service :- "On a day late in returning from leave to England."	
" "	7-11-17		N° T.T. 03230 Pte G. Sayles A.V.C. returned from leave in England.	
" "	7-11-17		N° SE 12852 Pte A.J. Every A.V.C. returned from leave in England.	
" "	7-11-17		N° T.T. 03163 W/A/LCpl S. Downing A.V.C. reduced to the ranks for the following offence. Drunkenness. Authority T.G.R.O.	
" "	9-11-17		N° T.T. 03230 Pte G. Sayles A.V.C. awarded 14 days F.P. N°. 1 for the following offence :- Whilst on Active Service "Overstaying leave to England by 5 days".	
" "	12-11-17		Senior vet Billets at Stinwoorde and proceeded to OUDERDOM areas to relieve 2nd Can. Field Am. M.V.S.	
" "	16-11-17		N° T.T. 03203 Pte S. Fawley A.V.C. admitted to 1/2 (WR) Field Ambulance	
" "	14-11-17		N° 562 Sergt. M.A. Ward A.V.C. and N° SE 3983 Pte G. Todd A.V.C. proceeded on leave to England. Leave granted from 15-11-17 to 29-11-17.	

WAR DIARY
or
INTELLIGENCE SUMMARY.
(Erase heading not required.)

Army Form C. 2118.

Place	Date	Hour	Summary of Events and Information	Remarks and references to Appendices
In the Field	19-11-17		No SE.12852 Pte. A.J. Every A.V.C. admitted to 2(WR) Field Ambulance evacuated to C.C.S. 22-11-17.	
" "	24-11-17		T/03163 Pte J. Dunning A.V.C. admitted to 2(WR) Field Ambulance. Transferred to H.q WR Divisional Rest Station 24-11-17. Sick vacation granted at 4 Inf. B.O.S. and moved to Remount.	
" "	26-11-17		No TT/03161 Sgt. E. Bradley. A.V.C. admitted to 2(WR) Field Ambulance. Transferred to H.q (WR) Divisional Rest Station 26-11-17.	
" "	28-11-17		No SE 21605 Pte A.G. Lawrence A.V.C. and SE 14184 Pte E.A. Jackson A.V.C. proceeded on leave to England. Leave granted from 19-11-17 to 3-12-17.	
" "	30-11-17		No SE 3983 Pte G. Todd A.V.C. returned from leave in England. During the month 344 Animals have been admitted to the Section and have been dealt with as follows. Transferred to B.van 251. Discharged to duty 80. 11 Died & Destroyed 8. Remaining under treatment 74.	

J. Price
O.C. 1st W.R. MOBILE VETERINARY SECTION.

Sgt

War Diary   Vol 31

"WR. Kurt Von Seck

January /18

WAR DIARY
or
INTELLIGENCE SUMMARY.
(Erase heading not required.)

Army Form C. 2118.

Place	Date	Hour	Summary of Events and Information	Remarks and references to Appendices
	2.1.18		47 horses and 3 mules evacuated to No 23 Veterinary Hospital. A special Veterinary Hospital was established at RENINGHELST for cases of Ophthalmia, when all animals suffering from specific ophthalmia were sent, instead of being treated in their own transport lines. One man per two animals & has was sent by each unit sending animals here, and has now were accommodation and rations by this section. 52 cases were admitted, and were disposed of as follows:- Evacuated to Base Veterinary Hospitals 34. Cases sent back to units 18.	MOBILE VETERINARY SECTION CAPTAIN, A.V.C.
10.	7.18		Horses and mules inspected at Veterinary Hospital, RENINGHELST to ascertain fitness.	
12.	1.18		The Section moved from RENINGHELST to at HONDEGHEM NORD (U6a98, sheet 27) The horses etc were quite fresh were quite fresh 12 horses and 3 mules were held over to the	

Army Form C. 2118.

WAR DIARY
INTELLIGENCE SUMMARY
(Erase heading not required.)

Place	Date	Hour	Summary of Events and Information	Remarks and references to Appendices
	18.1.18		Assumed command Mobile Veterinary Section.	
			Orders received through D.A.D.V.S. 49th (W.R.) Division from A.D.V.S. 22nd Corps for a return regarding by G.H.Q. showing the categories of the personnel of this section.	
	19.1.18		42 horses and 1 mule evacuated to No. 23 Veterinary Hospital by train.	
	22.1.18		3 horses and 1 mule evacuated to No. 23 Veterinary Hospital by motor ambulance.	
	23.1.18		2 horses evacuated to No. 23 Veterinary hospital by motor ambulance.	
			23 horses and 1 mule evacuated to No. 23 Veterinary Hospital by train.	
	26.1.18		20 horses and 7 mules evacuated to No. 23 Veterinary Hospital by train.	
	31.1.18		1 horse and 1 mule evacuated to No. 23 Veterinary Hospital by motor ambulance.	

WAR DIARY or INTELLIGENCE SUMMARY

Army Form C. 2118.

Place	Date	Hour	Summary of Events and Information	Remarks and references to Appendices
			The standard of efficiency of the category "B" men who have replaced the category "A" men dispatched to Base, is poor. They are not trained in Life duties, and are simply drones or men appointed with no knowledge of symptoms of diseases. In addition some are unable to undertake the increased work devolved upon men on outbreak from the Base, for in the evacuation and collection of sick animals, it is absolutely essential for men to be of good physique. It is no excuse for them to be turned into Mobile Veterinary Section - neither have the men received any instruction in the war of sick.	

O.C. 1/1 W.R. MOBILE VETERINARY SECTION. CAPTAIN. A.V.C.

WAR DIARY or INTELLIGENCE SUMMARY

Army Form C. 2118.

175 medical surgical cases were admitted during the month of January 1918, and 110 cases of ophthalmia.

277 animals have been evacuated to Base.

64 animals have been cured and discharged to duty.

3 animals have been destroyed.

[signature]
Captain A.V.C.
O.C. 1/1 W.R. Mobile Veterinary Section.

"War Diary" Ya 32
of
1/1 Wervicksing but Ver Seer
for
February 1918

Army Form C. 2118.

WAR DIARY
or
INTELLIGENCE SUMMARY.
(Erase heading not required.)

Instructions regarding War Diaries and Intelligence Summaries are contained in F. S. Regs., Part II. and the Staff Manual respectively. Title pages will be prepared in manuscript.

Place	Date	Hour	Summary of Events and Information	Remarks and references to Appendices
Field	1.2.18	5	medical and surgical cases evacuated. 10 medical and surgical cases and 10 ophthalmia cases evacuated by train to No. 23 Veterinary Hospital, St. Omer.	
	2.2.18	1	medical and surgical case and 3 ophthalmia cases admitted.	
	3.2.18	1	medical and surgical case and 1 ophthalmia case admitted.	
	4.2.18		medical and surgical cases admitted.	
	5.2.18	11	medical and surgical cases admitted.	
	6.2.18	10	medical and surgical cases and 6 ophthalmia cases evacuated by train to No. 23 Veterinary Hospital, St. Omer.	
	7.2.18		General Officer Veterinary and the recovery of ophthalmia.	
	8.2.18	3	medical and surgical cases and 3 ophthalmia cases admitted.	CAPTAIN, A.O.C. O.C. 4th W.R. MOBILE VETERINARY SECTION
	9.2.18	5	medical and surgical cases to ophthalmia cases and 5 ophthalmia cases evacuated by train to No. 23 Veterinary Hospital, St. Omer.	
	10.2.18	3	medical and surgical cases and 1 ophthalmia case admitted. No. 3 E.3602 Pte. EGGLETON B. despatched to No. 2 Veterinary Hospital.	

WAR DIARY or INTELLIGENCE SUMMARY

Army Form C. 2118.

Place	Date	Hour	Summary of Events and Information	Remarks and references to Appendices
Field			Hospital shown to working travel for replacement as required. A.V.C. with a Brigade on Relay.	
	11.2.18		2 medical and surgical cases admitted	
	12.2.18		2 medical and surgical cases admitted. And 2 medical and surgical cases evacuated to No. 23 Veterinary Hospital. St. Omer by motor ambulance. 1 man proceeded on leave.	
	13.2.18		3 medical and surgical cases and 2 ophthalmic cases admitted. 8 medical and surgical cases and 6 ophthalmic cases evacuated by motor to No. 23 Veterinary Hospital St. Omer.	
	14.2.18		1 surgical case admitted. General officer commanding veterinary weekly returns.	
	15.2.18		5 medical and surgical cases and 2 ophthalmic cases admitted. 2 surgical cases evacuated by motor ambulance to No. 23 Veterinary Hospital. No cases remained.	
	16.2.18		4 medical and surgical cases admitted.	

Army Form C. 2118.
Sheet No. 3

WAR DIARY
or
INTELLIGENCE SUMMARY.
(Erase heading not required.)

Instructions regarding War Diaries and Intelligence Summaries are contained in F. S. Regs., Part II. and the Staff Manual respectively. Title pages will be prepared in manuscript.

Place	Date	Hour	Summary of Events and Information	Remarks and references to Appendices
Lille	16.2.18		9 horses and 2 mules cast by D.D.R. General Army sent to No. 23 Veterinary Hospital St Omer.	
	17.2.18		4 horses and 2 mules cast by D.D.R. General Army admitted.	
	18.2.18		2 medical and surgical cases and 1 ophthalmic case admitted. 8 medical and surgical cases and 1 ophthalmic case and 6 animals cast by D.D.R. evacuated to No. 23 Veterinary Hospital St Omer.	
				By W.M. MOBILE VETERINARY SECTION, CARTON, A.V.C.
	20.2.18		to S.E. No. 110 P.M.Veterinary Section arrived as a reinforcement from No. 19 Veterinary Hospital. 5 medical and surgical cases and 1 ophthalmic case admitted. 3 ophthalmic cases evacuated to No. 23 Veterinary Hospital St Omer.	
	21.2.18		14 medical and surgical cases and 1 ophthalmic case admitted. 21 medical and surgical cases and 3 ophthalmic cases evacuated by road to St Omer. 4 medical and surgical cases sent by veterinary ambulance to No. 23 Veterinary Hospital St Omer.	

Army Form C. 2118.

WAR DIARY
or
INTELLIGENCE SUMMARY.
(Erase heading not required.)

Instructions regarding War Diaries and Intelligence Summaries are contained in F. S. Regs., Part II. and the Staff Manual respectively. Title pages will be prepared in manuscript.

Place	Date	Hour	Summary of Events and Information	Remarks and references to Appendices
Field	21.2.18		Three remounts were received, of weekly returns.	
	24.2.18		The section moved from HONDEGHEM NORD (M.6.b.9.8. sheet 27) to WALKERS CAMP (H.27.b.6.9. sheet 28)	
	27.2.18		6 received and evacuated 2 Ipplepen case admitted	
	28.2.18	16	11 mules and one injured case and 4 Ipplepen cases admitted. During the month of February 10 horses and 6 mules have been discharged to duty. 1 horse has died, one horse has been destroyed.	

R. Hutch
Captain A.V.C.
O.C. No. 41 W. R. Mobile Veterinary Section.

Vol 33

War Diary
of
1/1 (W.R.) M.V.S. 49 Division
for
the month of March 1918.

Army Form C. 2118.

WAR DIARY
or
INTELLIGENCE SUMMARY.
(Erase heading not required.)

Instructions regarding War Diaries and Intelligence Summaries are contained in F. S. Regs., Part II, and the Staff Manual respectively. Title pages will be prepared in manuscript.

Place	Date	Hour	Summary of Events and Information	Remarks and references to Appendices
In the Field	23-2-18		1 Horse suffering from Bomb Wounds (General) evacuated to XXII Corps VCCS by Horse Ambulance.	
"	3-3-18		1 Horse suffering from Gunshot Wounds evacuated to VCCS by Horse Ambulance	
"	1-3-18		No SE 12852 Pte A.J. Every A.V.C. reported for duty from No 9 MVS	
"	5-3-18		Notification received that No 562 Sergt M.A Ward AVC evacuated Sick to Base	
"	7-3-18		45 Horses 5 Mules evacuated to Base through XXII Corps VCCS.	
"	8-3-18		No TT 03171 Sergt-aH Heroninghan AVC provided on leave to England — Leave granted from 9-3-18 to 23-3-18	
"	12-3-18		No TT 027 Staff-Sergt- E.L Rolf AVC provided to XXII Corps VCCS for duty Authority ADVS XXII Corps 15/43 of 9-3-18	
"	13-3-18		LT 02216 Sergt- F.J.S Taylor AVC temporarily attached 1(UR) MVS for duty 41 Horses 2 Mules evacuated to Base through Corps VCCS (XXII)	
"	14-3-18		1 Horse suffering from Gunshot Wounds evacuated to XXII Corps VCCS 34 Horses and 1 Mule evacuated to Base through XXII Corps VCCS	
"	19-3-18		No 5296 Sergt- B Winter AVC reported for duty from the Base on relief of No 562 Sergt M.A Ward AVC evacuated to England	
"	20-3-18			
"	23-3-18		1 Horse suffering from Gunshot Wounds evacuated to XXII Corps VCCS by Ambulance	

Army Form C. 2118.

WAR DIARY
or
INTELLIGENCE SUMMARY.
(Erase heading not required.)

Place	Date	Hour	Summary of Events and Information	Remarks and references to Appendices
Nr Fatah W 26.3.18			N° TT 03171 Sergt. A.H. Denning from AVC reports back from leave in England	
"	27-3-18		1 Horse suffering from Gunshot-Wound of Neck evacuated to VCCS by Ambulance	
"	28-3-18		1 Horse suffering from Puncture wound of Neck felt evacuated to VCCS by Ambulance	
"	28-3-18		16 horse Mules evacuated to Base through Corps VCCS.	
"	29-3-18		N° TT 03216 Sergt F.J.S Taylor AVC returned to his Unit.	
"	29-3-18		N° 8536 Pte S.R Thickman AVC admitted into Private AVC admitted 1/2 (NR) Field Ambulance. During this month two Privates AVC have been sent to this Corps School of Sanitation for a course of instruction	

P. Price
CAPTAIN, A.V.C.
O.C. 111 W.R. MOBILE VETERINARY SECTION

WAR DIARY

OF
1/1st (W.R.) Mob. Vet. Sec.

FOR MONTH OF
APRIL 1918

Army Form C. 2118.

WAR DIARY
or
INTELLIGENCE SUMMARY
(Erase heading not required.)

Instructions regarding War Diaries and Intelligence Summaries are contained in F.S. Regs., Part II. and the Staff Manual respectively. Title Pages will be prepared in manuscript.

Place	Date	Hour	Summary of Events and Information	Remarks and references to Appendices
In the field	3-4-18		Section vacated Billets at Walker Camp and proceeded to Westoutre where Billets were taken up in Conqueror Camp. Billets and horse-lines at Walker Camp, were handed over to the 6" Division M.V.S. also 25 Horses and 5 Mules - unfit to march - with the Section.	O.C. 11 N.Z. Mobile Veterinary Section. Captain, A.V.C. [signature]
"	10-4-18		46 Horses and 4 Mules evacuated to Corps V.E.S	
"	10-4-18		Ptes. Oldfield - Edwards - Britt and Parris returned to this Section from the Corps V.E.S. having been attached to that Unit for duty.	
"	11-4-18		Section vacated Billets at Conqueror Camp. Billets and horse lines taken over at Kenora Camp on the Runninghilst - Westoutre Road.	
"	11-4-18		2 Horses evacuated to Corps V.E.S.	
"	13-4-18		No. 7710 P/A/ Corporal. F. COLES A.V.C. despatched to No. 2 Veterinary Hospital to undergo further training and examination for appointment as P/A/ Sergt. A.V.C to a Field Unit. (Authority O.1/AVC Base Records T10/152/184/104-18)	
"	16-4-18	9pm	A Battery of 6" Howitzers took up a position in this Section horse lines but did not commence firing until mid-day 17".	

2449 Wt. W14957/M90 750,000 1/16 J.B.C. & A. Forms/C.2118/12.

Army Form C. 2118.

WAR DIARY
or
INTELLIGENCE SUMMARY

(Erase heading not required.)

Instructions regarding War Diaries and Intelligence Summaries are contained in F.S. Regs., Part II. and the Staff Manual respectively. Title Pages will be prepared in manuscript.

Place	Date	Hour	Summary of Events and Information	Remarks and references to Appendices
In the Field	17-4-18		Section moved to Conqueror Camp	
"	18-4-18		1 Horse evacuated by Ambulance to Corps V.E.S at Wippenhoek	
"	18-4-18		Owing to the heavy shelling of Westoutre the "Conqueror Camp" was vacated and Billets and Horse-lines were taken up in a field near Abeele.	
"	19-4-18		20 Horses and 1 Mule admitted and evacuated to Corps V.E.S at Wippenhoek	
"	22-4-18		Section vacated Billets and Horse lines near Abeele – New location K 35 d 7.2. (Sheet 27) on the ABEELE STEENVOORDE Road.	
"	24-4-18		1 Horse evacuated to Corps V.E.S by Ambulance.	
"	25-4-18		5 Horses evacuated to Corps V.E.S by Ambulance.	
"	26-4-18		11 Horses 1 Mule evacuated to Corps V.E.S	
"	26-4-18		6 Horses evacuated to Corps V.E.S by Ambulance	
"	27-4-18		13 Horses 1 Mule evacuated by road to VIII Corps V.E.S for Walking cases near Hondeghem.	
"	29-4-18		1 Horse evacuated to Corps V.E.S by Ambulance	
"	30-4-18		12 Horses and 11 Mules evacuated to V.E.S at Proven of which 8 were evacuated by Ambulance	
"			During the month the personnel of this Section have received instruction in the use of the Rifle – Riding exercises and Drill.	

P. Rea
CAPTAIN, A.V.C.

Vol. 35

1 War Diary of
11 (WR) Inv Vet Sec
for
May 1918

Army Form C. 2118.

WAR DIARY
or
INTELLIGENCE SUMMARY.
(Erase heading not required.)

Instructions regarding War Diaries and Intelligence Summaries are contained in F. S. Regs., Part II. and the Staff Manual respectively. Title pages will be prepared in manuscript.

Place	Date	Hour	Summary of Events and Information	Remarks and references to Appendices
In the Field	1.5.18		13 Horses evacuated to No 22 V.E.S. Proven & Cpl Clarkson, 3 men.	
"	2.5.18		2 Horses and 3 Mules evacuated to No 8 V.E.S. at Hondeghem	
"	3.5.18		Senior visited Billets on the Steenvoorde - Abeele Road and provided to a field on the Steenvoorde - Watou Road.	
"	5.5.18		1 Mule 5 Horses conveyed by Ambulance to No 22 V.E.S. Proven	
"	5.5.18		7 Horses 6 Mules evacuated to No 8 V.E.S. Hondeghem	
"	7.5.18		8 Horses evacuated to No 8 V.E.S. Hondeghem	
"	7.5.18		1 Horse conveyed by Ambulance to No 22 V.E.S. Proven	
"	8.5.18		7 Horses 1 Mule evacuated to No 8 V.E.S.	
"	9.5.18		1 Horse conveyed by Ambulance to No 22 V.E.S. Proven	
"	9.5.18		Senior visited Billets in the Steenvoorde - Watou road and proceeded to SCHOOLS CAMP on the Poperinghe - Watou Road	
"	11.5.18		4 Horses conveyed by Ambulance to No 22 V.E.S. Proven	
"	13.5.18		8 Horses 1 Mule evacuated to No 8 V.E.S. Hondeghem	
"	13.5.18		4 Horses evacuated to No 22 V.E.S.	
"	15.5.18		3 Horses evacuated to No 22 V.E.S. Proven	

O.C. 1/1 W.R. MOBILE VETERINARY SECTION.
CAPTAIN A.V.C.

WAR DIARY
INTELLIGENCE SUMMARY

Army Form C. 2118.

Place	Date	Hour	Summary of Events and Information	Remarks and references to Appendices
	17-5-18		The following NCO and men were transferred to No 22 V.E.S. Brown owing to the reduction in the War Establishment of a Mobile Veterinary Section :- No T.T. 027 Staff-Sergt E.L. RELF AVC - No 7020 Pte W.T. EDWARDS AVC No 4826 Pte D. OLDFIELD AVC - T.T. 02436 Pte H. HARRIS AVC Struck off Section Strength with effect from 17-5-18	
	17-5-18		Notification received from O.C. No 22 V.E.S. that No 32165 Pte H. BRITT AVC had been transferred to No 2 Veterinary Hospital - Struck off Section Strength	
	18-5-18		No SE 770 (P/A) Corporal F. COLES AVC was returned to the Section from No 2 Veterinary Hospital having been sent there in the previous month to undergo further training and examination for appointment as a Sergt AVC to a Field Unit. Taken on Section Strength with effect from 18-5-18	
	19-5-18		3 Horses transferred to No 22 V.E.S. Brown.	
	20-5-18		Under authority of ADVS II Corps the following men were transferred to No 2 V.E.S. Brown being surplus to the New War Establishment of a M.V.S.	

Army Form C. 2118.

WAR DIARY
or
INTELLIGENCE SUMMARY.
(Erase heading not required.)

Place	Date	Hour	Summary of Events and Information	Remarks and references to Appendices
	18-5-18		No 12390 Pte T.B. HOWLETT A.V.C. — No 14184 Pte E.A.L. JACKSON A.V.C. No 29390 Pte T.H. MAGGS A.V.C. — No 30479 Pte J.W. ANDERSON A.V.C. A.D.V.S. 17 Cats arrived and inspect Sulieu lines also Johnson Equipment.	
	21-5-18		3 Horses 5 Mules evacuated to No 22 V.E.S. Brown. 1 Horse conv by Ambulance	
	23-5-18		13 Horses 1 Mule evacuated to No 22 V.E.S. Brown.	
	25-5-18		No T.T. 03268 Pte H. SYKES A.V.C. transferred to No 2 V.E.S. having become surplus to the Section Establishment owing to the return of No 770 P/A/Corporal F. COLES A.V.C.	
	25-5-18		10 Horses 3 Mules evacuated to No 22 V.E.S. Brown.	
	27-5-18		Horse conveyed by Ambulance to No 22 V.E.S. Brown	
	28-5-18		4 Horses evacuated to No 22 V.E.S. Brown.	
	31-5-18		2 Horses conveyed by Ambulance to No 22 V.E.S. Brown.	
	31-5-18		5 Horses evacuated to No 22 V.E.S. Brown	

S.S.&N. W.R. MOBILE VETERINARY SECTION
CAPTAIN, A.V.C.

War Diary

1/1 (UR)
Hq (UR) Division

for the month of
June. 1918.

Army Form C. 2118.

WAR DIARY
or
INTELLIGENCE SUMMARY
(Erase heading not required.)

Place	Date	Hour	Summary of Events and Information	Remarks and references to Appendices
In the field	1-6-18		3 Horses admitted to the Section	
" "	2-6-18		One L.S. horse - #Q 245(WR) Bde RFA suffering from Gas Poisoning (Pneumonia) Conveyed by Ambulance to this Section	
" "	2-6-18		10 Horses 1 Mule admitted to the Section	
" "	2-6-18		6 Horses evacuated to No 22 V.E.S., one conveyed by Ambulance	
" "	3-6-18		2 Horses evacuated to No 2 V.E.S. by Ambulance	
" "	3-6-18		1 Horse collected by Ambulance from H.Q. 49 (WR) Div. and taken direct to No 2 V.E.S.	
" "	3-6-18		9 Horses 1 Mule evacuated to No 2 V.E.S.	
" "	4-6-18		Section vacated School Camp L 3 d 8.4 (Sheet 7) and proceeded to Pitchcott Camp. F 8 d 3.7 (Sheet 27)	
" "	4-6-18		2 Horses conveyed by Ambulance from old to new location	
" "	4-6-18		1 Horse 1 Mule admitted to Section	
" "	6-6-18		1 Horse admitted to Section — 1 Horse 1 Mule evacuated to No 22 V.E.S.	
" "	7-6-18		4 Horses admitted to the Section	
" "	7-6-18		D.A.D.V.S. inspected animals for evacuation	
" "	7-6-18		1 Mule collected by Ambulance from 11th B.A.C. Army F.A. Bde.	

WAR DIARY or INTELLIGENCE SUMMARY

Army Form C. 2118.

Place	Date	Hour	Summary of Events and Information	Remarks and references to Appendices
In the Field	8-6-18		6 Horses admitted to the Section. 1 Horse evacuated by Ambulance to No 22 V.E.S. 1 Horse collected by Ambulance from D/112 Batty R.F.A. 6" Division.	
" "	8-6-18		5 Horses evacuated to No 22 V.E.S.	
" "	10-6-18		3 Horses admitted to the Section.	
" "	10-6-18		2 Horses evacuated to No 22 V.E.S, one conveyed by Ambulance. Cast-book No 238 Stray Mule discharged to duty to No 1 Section 149(HR) D.A.C.	
" "	11-6-18		1 Horse admitted to the Section.	
" "	12-6-18		Cast-book No 258 Stray L.D. Horse discharged to duty to A/246(WR) Batty R.F.A. 7 Horses, 1 Mule admitted to the Section	
" "	12-6-18		6 Horses, 1 Mule evacuated to No 22 V.E.S.	
" "	12-6-18		Cast-book No 262 Mule 11th B.A.C. Army F.A. Bde. destroyed. P.M. revealed Fracture of N Radius.	
" "	12-6-18		Two grey Geldings L.D. strays discharged to duty to D/245(WR) Batty R.F.A.	
" "	13-6-18		1 Mule conveyed by Ambulance to No 22 V.E.S.	
" "	13-6-18		Influenza occurred in the Section. The following NCO and men were admitted to 1/3(WR) Field Ambulance suffering from Pyrexia. No S.E. 5296 Sergt B. WINTER A.V.C - SE 12852 Pte A.S./EVERY A.V.C - SE 6536 Pte T. ELDRIDGE A.V.C. No SE 8836 Pte S.R. HICKMAN A.V.C	O.C. 1/1 N.R MOBILE VETERINARY SECTION. CAPTAIN, A.V.C.

Army Form C. 2118.

WAR DIARY
or
INTELLIGENCE SUMMARY

(Erase heading not required.)

Instructions regarding War Diaries and Intelligence Summaries are contained in F.S. Regs., Part II. and the Staff Manual respectively. Title Pages will be prepared in manuscript.

Place	Date	Hour	Summary of Events and Information	Remarks and references to Appendices
In the Field	13-6-18		1 Horse, 1 Mule admitted to the Section.	
" "	14-6-18		1 Horse, 1 Mule admitted to the Section	
" "	14-6-18		1 Horse evacuated to No. 22 V.E.S. by Ambulance	
" "	15-6-18		6 Horses, 2 Mules evacuated to No. 22 V.E.S. — 1 Mule, 1 Horse conveyed by Ambulance	
" "	15-6-18		No. 5296 Sergt. T.B. WINTER. A.V.C. — No. 8836 Pte. S.R. HICKMAN A.V.C discharged to duty from Hospital	
" "	15-6-18		3 Horses admitted to the Section	
" "	16-6-18		No. 770317 3 Pte (L/Cpl) E. BATTY. A.V.C. — No. 12852 Pte A.J. EVERY A.V.C. — No. 3766 Pte A.H. HARRIS A.V.C. discharged to duty from Hospital	
" "	16-6-18		No. T4/249655 Dr. J. CAHILL A.S.C. — No. T4/249615 Dr. F. HARRISON A.S.C. admitted 1/2 (W.R) Field Ambulance — evacuated to C.C.S. and struck off the Section strength.	
" "	16-6-18		3 Horses admitted to the Section	
" "	17-6-18		Lieut-Colonel CONDER A.V.C. for D.D.V.S. Second Army accompanied by A.D.V.S. II Corps and D.A.D.V.S. visited Section and inspected animals for evacuation	
" "	17-6-18		4 Horses 1 Mule admitted to the Section	
" "	18-6-18		6 Horses, 1 Mule evacuated to No. 22 V.E.S. by Ambulance	
" "	18-6-18		No. SE 6536 Pte. T. ELDRIDGE A.V.C. discharged to duty from Hospital	
" "	18-6-18		2 Horses admitted to the Section	

Army Form C. 2118.

WAR DIARY
or
INTELLIGENCE SUMMARY

(Erase heading not required.)

Instructions regarding War Diaries and Intelligence Summaries are contained in F.S. Regs., Part II. and the Staff Manual respectively. Title Pages will be prepared in manuscript.

Place	Date	Hour	Summary of Events and Information	Remarks and references to Appendices
In the field	19-6-18		N°SE.13364 S.Smith W. BELSHAM A.V.C. – N°SE.1665 Pte. D. FRENCH A.V.C. – N° TT.0731 Pte. D.q. HEASMAN A.V.C.: admitted 1/3(WR) Field Ambulance.	
"	19-6-18		1 Horse evacuated to N°22 V.E.S. by Ambulance	
"	19-6-18		1 Horse admitted to this Section	
"	20-6-18		1 Mule collected by Ambulance from the 1/5 West York Regt.	
"	20-6-18		1 Mule, 1 Horse, conveyed by Ambulance to N°22 V.E.S.	
"	20-6-18		1 Horse evacuated to N°22 V.E.S.	
"	20-6-18		1 Horse collected by Ambulance from 112 Heavy Battery R.G.A.	
"	20-6-18		1 Horse 1 Mule admitted to this Section.	
"	21-6-18		Reduction of Horse establishment – (G.R.O. 4252 dated 11-6-18) 1 Horse transferred to 466 Coy A.S.C.	
"	21-6-18		2 Horses 4 Mules admitted to this Section	
"	22-6-18		3 Horses 5 Mules evacuated to N°22 V.E.S. (one horse conveyed by Ambulance)	
"	22-6-18		N°SE.1665 Pte. D. FRENCH. A.V.C. – N°TT.0731 Pte. D.q. HEASMAN A.V.C. discharged to duty from Hospital.	
"	23-6-18		1 Horse collected by Ambulance from D Batty 11th Bde Army F.A.	
"	23-6-18		N°SE.13364 S.Smith W. BELSHAM. A.V.C. discharged to duty from Hospital.	
"	23-6-18		5 Horses, 1 Mule admitted to this Section	
"	24-6-18		2 Horses admitted to this Section	
"	24-6-18		6 Horses 1 Mule evacuated to N°22 V.E.S. (one horse conveyed by Ambulance)	

Army Form C. 2118.

WAR DIARY
INTELLIGENCE SUMMARY

(Erase heading not required.)

Place	Date	Hour	Summary of Events and Information	Remarks and references to Appendices
In the Field	25-6-18		Cas-Cook No. 291 H.D. has discharged to duty to 463 Coy A.S.C.	
" "	25-6-18		2 Horses admitted to the Section	
" "	26-6-18		6 Horses evacuated to No. 22 V.E.S.	
" "	26-6-18		3 Horses admitted to the Section	
" "	26-6-18		Cas-Cook No. 285 Stray Riding horse discharged to duty to 1/5 West Yorks Regt.	
" "	26-6-18		Cas-Cook No. 288 - 9 H.D. horse despatched to Field Remount Section Army Artillery School TILQUES near St-Omer	
" "	28-6-18		2 Horses 2 Mules evacuated to No. 22 V.E.S.	
" "	28-6-18		1 Horse, 1 Mule admitted to the Section	
" "	28-6-18		Cas-Cook No. 243 Stray I.D. horse bearing the brand of the Belgian Army was returned to 2nd Corps de transport 2nd D.A. Belgian Army	
" "	29-6-18		1 Horse admitted to the Section	
" "	30-6-18		2 Horses evacuated to No. 22 V.E.S. (one have enveyed by Ambulance) Reduction in horse Establishment (G.R.O 4252 dated 11-6-18) 1 horse was issued to 463 Coy A.S.C.	

J.H.C.
Captain, A.V.C.
O.C. ? Mt. Mobile Veterinary Section

WO 37 49

A War Diary of
1/1 (W R) M.V.S
for the month of July
1918

WAR DIARY or INTELLIGENCE SUMMARY

Army Form C. 2118.

Place	Date	Hour	Summary of Events and Information	Remarks and references to Appendices
In the Field	1-7-18		2 Horses admitted to this Section	
" "	2-7-18		1 Mule collected by Ambulance from 11" B.A.C. Army F.A. Bde.	
" "	2-7-18		3 Horses, 2 Mules evacuated to No 22 V.E.S. (one horse conveyed by Ambulance)	M4708 AVC
" "	4-7-18		3 Horses, 3 Mules admitted evacuated to No 22 V.E.S. (2 Mules conveyed by Ambulance)	
" "	4-7-18		2 Horses, 1 Mule admitted to this Section	
" "	4-7-18		No T.T. 03171 Sergt. A.G. Heveningham A.V.C. awarded the Meritorious Service Medal (Auth: 2nd Supplement London Gazette dated 17-6-18)	1/c 1/1 W.R. Mobile Veterinary Section. "Captain, A.V.C."
" "	5-7-18		1 Horse admitted to this Section	
" "	6-7-18		Reduction in Horse Establishment (G.R.O. 4252 dated 11-6-18) 1 horse was issued to 57th Field Coy R.E.	
" "	6-7-18		8 Horses admitted to this Section	
" "	6-7-18		9 Horses evacuated to No 22 V.E.S. (one horse conveyed by Ambulance)	
" "	7-7-18		5 Horses 1 Mule admitted to this Section	
" "	7-7-18		1 Horse collected by Ambulance from 2nd Pontoon Park, R.E.	
" "	5-7-18		No T4/257045 S⁴. J.T. Conner A.S.C. reports for duty from #63 Coy A.S.C. to replace No T4/249615 S⁴. F.W. Harrison A.S.C. admitted to Hospital.	C.E. Peters
" "	8-7-18		5 Horses 1 Mule admitted to this Section	
" "	6-7-18		5 Horses 1 Mule evacuated to No 2 V.E.S. (one horse conveyed by Ambulance)	

Army Form C. 2118.

WAR DIARY
or
INTELLIGENCE SUMMARY

(Erase heading not required.)

Instructions regarding War Diaries and Intelligence Summaries are contained in F. S. Regs., Part II. and the Staff Manual respectively. Title Pages will be prepared in manuscript.

Place	Date	Hour	Summary of Events and Information	Remarks and references to Appendices
In the Field	8-7-18		1 Horse collected by Ambulance from 463 Coy A.S.C.	for MAJOR A.V.C. B.C. 1/1 W.R. MOBILE VETERINARY SECTION. CAPTAIN, A.V.C.
" "	9-7-18		2 Horses admitted to the Section	
" "	10-7-18		8 Horses 2 Mules admitted to the Section	
" "	10-7-18		11 Horses 1 Mule evacuated to No. 22 V.E.S.	
" "	11-7-18		1 Horse admitted to the Section	
" "	11-7-18		8 Horses 1 Mule admitted to the Section	
" "	12-7-18		9 Horses 1 Mule evacuated to No. 22 V.E.S. (one horse conveyed by Ambulance)	
" "	12-7-18		1 Mule evacuated by Ambulance from 1/7 W.R. Regt.	
" "	13-7-18		5 Horses 1 Mule admitted to the Section	
" "	14-7-18		5 Horses admitted to the Section	
" "	15-7-18		14 Horses admitted to the Section	
" "	15-7-18		15 Horses 2 Mules evacuated to No. 2 V.E.S. (2 Horses 1 Mule conveyed by Ambulance)	
" "	16-7-18		1 Horse collected by Ambulance from 1/7 Duke of Wellington Regt.	
" "	17-7-18		5 Horses admitted to the Section	
" "	18-7-18		1 Horse admitted to the Section	
" "	18-7-18		10 Horses evacuated to No. 2 V.E.S.	A.E. Jones

Army Form C. 2118.

WAR DIARY
or
INTELLIGENCE SUMMARY

(Erase heading not required.)

Place	Date	Hour	Summary of Events and Information	Remarks and references to Appendices
In the Field	20-7-18		6 Horses admitted to the Section.	
" "	21-7-18		4 Horses admitted to the Section.	
" "	21-7-18		8 Horses evacuated to No 2 V.E.S.	
" "	23-7-18		1 Horse admitted to the Section.	
" "	23-7-18		Cast-Cook No 380 Bay Geld'd discharged to duty to 1/7 West York Regt	
" "	24-7-18		Cast-Cook No 337 Brown Mule Geld. (Stray) discharged to duty to B.Coy 49 M.G. Batt.	
" "	24-7-18		5 Horses admitted to the Section	
" "	22-7-18		1 Horse / Mule evacuated to No 2 V.E.S.	
" "	25-7-18		4 Horses admitted to the Section	
" "	26-7-18		8 Horses evacuated to No 2 V.E.S	
" "	27-7-18		No T 4/257045 Driver J. NOONAN 463 Coy A.S.C. reported for duty to replace Driver J. CAHILL A.S.C.	
" "	27-7-18		2 Horses admitted to the Section	
" "	26-7-18		Cast. book No 357 Gry geld L.D. discharged to duty to 49 (WR) Signal Coy R.E.	
" "	28-7-18		Cast. book No 366 Black Geld. L.D. discharged to duty to 105 Coy Engineers 30th American Division.	
" "	29-7-18		5 Horses admitted to the Section.	
" "	30-7-18		7 Horses / Mule evacuated to No 2 V.E.S. (one horse conveyed by Ambulance)	

A. M. Foster
Capt. A.V.C.
MAJOR A.V.C.
W. R. MOBILE VETERINARY SECTION.

War Diary
of
1/1 (W R) M.V.S.
of 49 (W R) Division
for the month of August
1918

WAR DIARY
or
INTELLIGENCE SUMMARY

Army Form C. 2118.

(Erase heading not required.)

Place	Date	Hour	Summary of Events and Information	Remarks and references to Appendices
In the Field	2-8-18		7 Horses admitted to the Section	
"	3-8-18		3 Horses / Mule evacuated to No 2 V.E.S. (one Mule conveyed by Ambulance).	
"	4-8-18		1 Horse admitted to this Section	
"	5-8-18		4 Horses evacuated to No 2 V.E.S. (one horse conveyed by Ambulance)	
"	6-8-18		4 Horses admitted to the Section	
"	6-8-18		2 Stray L.D horses issued to A/246(WR) Batty RFA (with No. 49(WR) Division)	
"	7-8-18		5 Horses / Mule evacuated to No 2 V.E.S	
"	8-8-18		2 Horses admitted to the Section	
"	9-8-18		3 Horses admitted to this Section	
"	10-8-18		4 Horses evacuated to No 2 V.E.S.	
"	11-8-18		2 Horses / Mule admitted to the Section	
"	12-8-18		2 Horses / Mule evacuated to No 2 V.E.S.	
"	13-8-18		7 Horses / Mule admitted to the Section	
"	14-8-18		5 Horses evacuated to No 2 V.E.S	
"	14-8-18		2 L.D Horses (Stray) re-issued to 17th Regt de ligne Belgian Army	
"	10-8-18		2 H.D Horses discharged to duty to 139 Labour Coy II Corps	
"	10-8-18			

Army Form C. 2118.

WAR DIARY
or
INTELLIGENCE SUMMARY

(Erase heading not required.)

Instructions regarding War Diaries and Intelligence Summaries are contained in F. S. Regs., Part II. and the Staff Manual respectively. Title Pages will be prepared in manuscript.

Place	Date	Hour	Summary of Events and Information	Remarks and references to Appendices
In the field	11-8-16		Grey Gelding L.D. discharged to duty to No 2 Section Hq (WR) S.A.C.	
,,	11-8-16		Bay mare L.D. discharged to duty to 456 (WR) Field Coy R.E.	
,,	15-8-16		5 Horses 1 Mule admitted to the Section.	
,,	16-8-16		1 Horse 3 Mules evacuated to No 2 V.E.S.	
,,	16-8-16		2 Stray L-D Horses returned to 2 Coy 2nd Division Corps de Transport Belgian Army.	
,,	17-8-16		4 Horses 1 Mule admitted to the Section	
,,	17-8-16		2 Horses 1 Mule evacuated to No 2 V.E.S.	
,,	18-8-16		4 Horses evacuated to No 2 V.E.S	
,,	19-8-16		1 Horse 1 Mule admitted to the Section	
,,	19-8-16		1 Horse 3 Mules evacuated to No 2 V.E.S.	
,,	19-8-16		No 5234 Pte W WRIGHT AVC and No 31500 Pte A McQUARRIE AVC reported for duty from No 2 V.H.	
,,	20-8-16		Brown gelding discharged to 465 Coy ASC	
,,	20-8-16 5am		Section evacuated PITCHCOTT Camp and proceeded to LEDERZEELE via HERZEELE - WORMHOUDT - ESQUELBECQ - ZEGGERS CAPPEL - BROXEELE	
,,	21-8-16 8am		Section marched from LEDERZEELE to MUNCQ NIEURLET via WATTEN and EPERLECQUES.	
,,	25-8-16		No TT.03232 Pte E BANKS AVC and No TT.03230 Pte G SAYLES AVC despatched to No 2 Veterinary Hospital to undergo medical inspection, and if found fit to be transferred to Infantry. (Authority VO/C A.V.C Base Records No 20/1800/18 dated 13/8/16)	

S.C. IN W-R MOBILE VETERINARY SECTION
CAPTAIN, A.V.C.

WAR DIARY
or
INTELLIGENCE SUMMARY

Army Form C. 2118.

Place	Date	Hour	Summary of Events and Information	Remarks and references to Appendices
Nr Helfaut	26-8-18	1-30pm	Section marched from MUNCQ-NIEURLET to HELFAUT via ST MARTIN-AU-LAERT and WIZERNES.	
" "	27-8-18	6am	Section marched from HELFAUT to AMETTES via THEROUANNE and ESTREE-BLANCHE	
" "	28-8-18	6am	Section marched from AMETTES to ROUELLECOURT via PERNES and, ST POL.	
" "	30-8-18		8 Horses admitted to the Section	
" "	31-8-18		6 Horses 1 Mule admitted to the Section	
" "	31-8-18		12 Horses 1 Mule evacuated to No 22 V.E.S. at SIEVAL.	

CAPTAIN, A.V.C.
O/C 4th W. R. MOBILE VETERINARY SECTION.

49

WR 39

War Diary
of
1/1ˢᵗ (WR) M.V.S
49ᵗʰ (West Riding) Division
for the month of
September 1918.

WAR DIARY
or
INTELLIGENCE SUMMARY

Army Form C. 2118.

Place	Date	Hour	Summary of Events and Information	Remarks and references to Appendices
In the Field	1-9-18	8 pm	Section marched from ROELLE COURT to AGNIERES via TINQUES and AUBIGNY	
" "	3-9-18		1 Mule / Horse admitted to the Section	
" "	4-9-18		3 Horses admitted to the Section	
" "	5-9-18		2 Horses admitted to the Section	
" "	5-9-18		6 Horses 1 Mule evacuated to No 18 V.E.S. at FREVIN CAPELLE	
" "	7-9-18		6 Horses admitted to the Section	
" "	7-9-18		4 Horses evacuated to No 18 V.E.S.	
" "	8-9-18		4 Horses admitted to the Section	
" "	9-9-18		4 Horses admitted to the Section	
" "	9-9-18		10 Horses evacuated to No 18 V.E.S.	
" "	11-9-18		1 Horse 3 Mules admitted to the Section	
" "	11-9-18		1 Horse 2 Mules evacuated to No 18 V.E.S. Horse Ambulance evacuating Cases from R.V.E.S. to Railhead	
" "	12-9-18		4 Horses admitted to the Section	
" "	12-9-18		2 Horses 1 Mule evacuated to No 18 V.E.S.	
" "	13-9-18		2 Horses 1 Mule admitted to the Section	
" "	13-9-18		5 Horses 1 Mule evacuated to No 18 V.E.S. Horse Ambulance carrying Cases from 18 V.E.S. to Railhead	
" "	13-9-18		No.S.E. 776 Corporal F. Coles A.V.C. temporarily attached H.Q. 146 Infantry Bde., as a relief for Sergt. Whitehead A.V.C. proceeding on leave to England.	

Army Form C. 2118.

WAR DIARY
or
INTELLIGENCE SUMMARY

(Erase heading not required.)

Instructions regarding War Diaries and Intelligence Summaries are contained in F.S. Regs., Part II. and the Staff Manual respectively. Title Pages will be prepared in manuscript.

Place	Date	Hour	Summary of Events and Information	Remarks and references to Appendices
In the Field	14-9-18		Section marched from AGNIERES to ECOIVRES.	
"	15-9-18		3 Horses admitted to the Section.	
"	15-9-18		No. TT 03193 Corporal F. Clarkson A.V.C. proceeded on leave to England, leave granted from 16-9-18 to 30-9-18.	
			Section location from AGNIERES to ECOIVRES	
"	16-9-18		3 Horses evacuated to No. 18 V.E.S.	
"	17-9-18		8 Horses admitted to the Section. Horse Ambulance conveying cases from 18 V.E.S. to Railhead	
"	18-9-18		9 Horses 2 Mules admitted to the Section	
"	18-9-18		12 Horses evacuated to No. 18 V.E.S.	
"	19-9-18		5 Mules admitted to the Section.	
"	19-9-18		6 Horses 2 Mules evacuated to No. 18 V.E.S.	
"	20-9-18		4 Horses admitted to the Section. Horse Ambulance conveying cases from 18 V.E.S. to Railhead	
"	20-9-18		No. SE 8836 Private S.R. Stickman A.V.C. proceeded on leave to England, leave granted from 21-9-18 to 5-10-18	
"	21-9-18		2 Horses admitted to the Section	
"	21-9-18		9 Horses evacuated to No. 18 V.E.S.	
"	22-9-18		5 Horses 1 Mule admitted to the Section	
"	22-9-18		No. SE 13364 Shoeing Smith W. Belsham A.V.C. proceeded on leave to England, leave granted from 23-9-18 to 7-10-18	

WAR DIARY
or
INTELLIGENCE SUMMARY
(Erase heading not required.)

Army Form C. 2118.

Place	Date	Hour	Summary of Events and Information	Remarks and references to Appendices
In the Field	23-9-18		One Stray horse admitted to this Section, brought in by 341 Railway Construction Coy RE (5th)	
	24-9-18		Horse Ambulance carrying Cases from 18 V.E.S. to Railhead.	
	25-9-18		No. 1 T 03173 Pte (Acting) Q Batt. A.V.C. provided on leave to England, leave granted from 26-9-18 to 10-10-18.	
	25-9-18		14 Horse, 1 Mule evacuated to No. 18 V.E.S.	
	26-9-18		1 Horse, 2 Mules admitted to this Section	
	27-9-18		4 Horses admitted to this Section	
	27-9-18		7 Horses, 2 Mules admitted to the Section. Horse Ambulance to No. 18 V.E.S.	
	28-9-18		1 Horse admitted to this Section	
	28-9-18		1 Horse evacuated by Ambulance to No. 18 V.E.S.	
	29-9-18		2 Horses, 2 Mules admitted to this Section	
	29-9-18		4 Horses evacuated to No. 18 V.E.S.	
	30-9-18		9 Horses admitted to this Section	
	30-9-18		11 Horses, 2 Mules evacuated to No. 18 V.E.S.	

CAPTAIN, A.V.C.
W.R. MOBILE VETERINARY SECTION

War Diary
of
1/1 (W.R.) M.V.S.
for the month of
October 1918

WAR DIARY or INTELLIGENCE SUMMARY

Army Form C. 2118.

Place	Date	Hour	Summary of Events and Information	Remarks and references to Appendices
	1918 October 1st		7 Horses were admitted to the Section.	
	2nd		7 Horses were admitted and 6 Horses were evacuated. Cpl. Chadwick returned from leave. Pte Nickels proceeded on leave. S.D.V.S. 'O' inspected M.V.S.	
	3rd		1 Horse admitted. 7 Horses were evacuated.	
	4th		7 Horses admitted.	
	5th		14 Horses and 2 mules admitted. 18 Horses & 2 mules evacuated.	
	6th		4 Horses admitted.	
	7th		8 Horses admitted. 6 Horses evacuated.	
	8th		1 Horse, 1 mule admitted. 7 Horses, 1 mule evacuated.	
	9th		Ambulance engaged at M.V.E. in conveying sick for evacuation to rail head. The Section moved to Chevigny. Pte Furnell proceeded on leave.	
	10th		Sgt Hevening horn reported sick & admitted to a Field Ambulance. Pte Harris proceeded on leave. The Section moved to Baralle, there.	
	11th		10 admitted. 3 Horses admitted. Engaged clearing up place.	
	12th		9 Horses were admitted. Chevron Aid Post established at Cambrai. L/Cpl [?] head & admitted at Cambrai pending arrival 17 V.E.S.	

WAR DIARY or INTELLIGENCE SUMMARY

Army Form C. 2118.

Place	Date	Hour	Summary of Events and Information	Remarks and references to Appendices
	October 12		The Section moved to Escardoeuvres	
	13"		45 Horses, 23 Mules were admitted. 13 Horses 4 mules to K.L. collecting depot at Cambrai awaiting arrival F.V.E.S.	
	14"		6 Horses, 1 mule admitted. 4 Horses, 1 mule to depot at Cambrai Pte Pilgrim reported to duty; on return Pte Bavin handed over to military authorities at the collecting depot Cambrai to V.E.S.	1
	15"		10 Horses, 1 mule admitted. 15 Horses, 1 mule to V.E.S.	
	16"		2 Horses admitted. 1 Horse evacuated	3
	17"		2 Horses admitted	
	18"		16 Horses, 3 mules admitted. 6 Horses, 2 mules evacuated	G.L
	19"		17 Horses, 6 mules admitted. 19 Horses, 4 mules evacuated	
	20"		2 Horses, 1 mule admitted. 9 Horses, 3 mules evacuated	
	21"		D.D.V.S. & 1 Army visited the Section. 11 Horses, 1 mule admitted.	
			Pte Handcroft proceeded on leave. 11 " 2 mules evacuated	
	22"		2 Horses evacuated. Pte Lawrence proceeded on special leave.	
	23"		29 Horses, 4 mules admitted. 1 Horse evacuated	
	24"		A.D.V.S. XX11 Corps visited the Section. 27 Horses, 4 mules evacuated	

WAR DIARY or INTELLIGENCE SUMMARY

Army Form C. 2118.

Place	Date	Hour	Summary of Events and Information	Remarks and references to Appendices
	October 24th		Lt. Harris & French returned from leave.	
	25th		2 Horses admitted. Lt. Glenn proceeded on leave.	
			Sec Bries proceeded to No 2 Veterinary Hospital.	
	26th		4 Horses, 1 mule admitted. 5 Horses, 1 mule evacuated. 1 Horse died	
	27th		No Section moved to Ivergny. 2 Horses admitted. 1 Horse evacuated	
	28th		1 Horse, 2 mules admitted. 4 Horses evacuated	
	29th		13 Horses, 1 mule admitted. 1 Horse destroyed. No Wright proceeded on leave	
	30th		No Section moved to Dusty. 9 Horses, 1 mule evacuated.	
	31st		6 Horses admitted	

Signed,
CAPTAIN, A.V.S.
29th W.R. MOBILE VETERINARY

War Diary of
111 (tor) M.V.S
for the month of
November. 1918.

Army Form C. 2118.

WAR DIARY
or
INTELLIGENCE SUMMARY.
(Erase heading not required.)

Instructions regarding War Diaries and Intelligence Summaries are contained in F. S. Regs., Part II. and the Staff Manual respectively. Title pages will be prepared in manuscript.

Place	Date	Hour	Summary of Events and Information	Remarks and references to Appendices
In the Field	1-11-18		12 Horses 3 Mules admitted to the Section.	
" "	2-11-18		2 Horses 1 Mule admitted to the Section	
" "	2-11-18		Case-Cock No. 814 Bay geld. to 6" Duke of Wellington Regt, destroyed, suffering from Wounds & shelter N3 O. Forearm.	
" "	2-11-18		13 Horses 2 Mules evacuated to Veterinary Evacuating Station	
" "	3-11-18		8 Horses 3 Mules admitted to the Section.	
" "	3-11-18		Case-Cock No. 806 Bay geld. R. suffering from Contusion of Hock, discharged to duty to 464 Coy A.S.C.	
" "	3-11-18		21 Horses 2 Mules evacuated to V.E.S.	
" "	4-11-18		1 Horse admitted to the Section	
" "	4-11-18		11 Horses 4 Mules evacuated to V.E.S	
" "	5-11-18		Section vacated Billets at Douchy and proceeded to Courcelles	
" "	6-11-18		2 Horses admitted to the Section	
" "	7-11-18		8 Horses 1 Mule admitted to the Section	
" "	8-11-18		13 Horses 1 Mule admitted to the Section	
" "	8-11-18		17 Horses 2 Mules evacuated to V.E.S.	

Army Form C. 2118.

WAR DIARY
or
INTELLIGENCE SUMMARY.
(Erase heading not required.)

Instructions regarding War Diaries and Intelligence Summaries are contained in F. S. Regs., Part II. and the Staff Manual respectively. Title pages will be prepared in manuscript.

Place	Date	Hour	Summary of Events and Information	Remarks and references to Appendices
Hesdigneul	9-11-18		Section moved Billets at Courcelles and proceeded to Wagonville	
"	9-11-18		No. SE 19578 Pte. R.E Hardstaff AVC reported back from leave in England	
"	9-11-18		1 Horse admitted to this Section	
"	9-11-18		6 Horses evacuated to V.E.S	
"	10-11-18		2 Horses admitted to the Section	
"	11-11-18		5 Horses admitted to the Section	
"	13-11-18		5 Horses admitted to the Section	
"	13-11-18		8 Horses evacuated to V.E.S	
"	13-11-18		Pte. Mann and Lawrence AVC reported back from leave in England	
"	14-11-18		Section evacuated Billets at Wagonville and proceeded to Chateau Bernieux	
"	15-11-18		at Roost Warendin	
"	15-11-18		DVS Coln visited Section	
"	15-11-18		6 Horses admitted to the Section	
"	16-11-18		16 Horses evacuated to V.E.S	
"	16-11-18		9 Horses and 1 Mule admitted to the Section	
"	16-11-18		Driver J. Yoell. A.S.C. proceeded on leave to England	
"	17-11-18		3 Horses admitted to this Section	

Army Form C. 2118.

WAR DIARY
or
INTELLIGENCE SUMMARY.
(Erase heading not required.)

Instructions regarding War Diaries and Intelligence Summaries are contained in F. S. Regs., Part II. and the Staff Manual respectively. Title pages will be prepared in manuscript.

Place	Date	Hour	Summary of Events and Information	Remarks and references to Appendices
In the field	18-11-18		No TT 0317 Sergt Aly Herewinglow A.V.C. reported for duty from No 2 Veterinary Hospital, taken on the strength of the Section 18-11-18.	
	18-11-18		No SE 5296 Sergt-B Winter A.V.C admitted 1/3 wr Field Ambulance and evacuated to 42 CCS the same day. Struck off the strength of the Section with effect from 18-11-18.	B.E.F. M R. Mobile Veterinary Section Captain, A.V.C
	18-11-18		6 Horses 1 Mule admitted to the Section.	
	18-11-18		13 Horses evacuated to No 18 V.E.S.	
	18-11-18		No SE 5234 Pte W.H Wright A.V.C reported back from leave in England	
	19-11-18		11 Horses 1 Mule evacuated to No 18 V.E.S.	
	20-11-18		10 Horses 1 Mule admitted to the Section	
	21-11-18		1 Mule admitted to the Section	
	22-11-18		1 Horse admitted to the Section	
	23-11-18		3 Horses 2 Mules admitted to the Section.	
	24-11-18		4 Horses admitted to the Section.	
	25-11-18		9 Horses 2 Mules evacuated to No 18 V.E.S.	
	26-11-18		1 Mule admitted to the Section	

Army Form C. 2118.

WAR DIARY
or
INTELLIGENCE SUMMARY.
(Erase heading not required.)

Place	Date	Hour	Summary of Events and Information	Remarks and references to Appendices
Km Urbilil	29-11-18		1 Horse admitted to the Section	
—	30-11-18		3 Horses 1 Mule admitted to the Section	

CAPTAIN, A.V.C.
MOBILE VETERINARY SECTION

H.Q.
49 (W.R.) Division

Herewith War Diary of 1/1 (WR) Mobile Veterinary Section for the month of December 1918. Please acknowledge receipt hereon.

> D.A.D.V.S.
> 49TH
> (W.R.) DIVISION.
> No.
> Date 4-1-19

Capt R
MAJOR A.V.C.
D.A.D.V.S 49TH (W.R.) DIVISION

WAR DIARY
or
INTELLIGENCE SUMMARY.
(Erase heading not required).

Army Form C. 2118.

Mob Vety Vol 43

Place	Date	Hour	Summary of Events and Information	Remarks and references to Appendices
Kut K	1-12-18		5 Horses 1 Mule admitted to the Section	
"	2-12-18		13 Horses admitted to the Section	
"	2-12-18		9 Horses 2 Mules evacuated to No 18 V.E.S	
"	3-12-18		11 Horses 9 Mules admitted to the Section	
"	4-12-18		8 Horses admitted to the Section	
"	4-12-18		23 Horses 9 Mules evacuated to No 18 V.E.S	
"	5-12-18		16 Horses admitted to the Section	
"	5-12-18		13 Horses evacuated to No 18 V.E.S	
"	6-12-18		24 Horses admitted to the Section	
"	6-12-18		12 Horses evacuated to No 18 V.E.S	
"	7-12-18		1 Horse admitted to the Section	
"	7-12-18		23 Horses evacuated to No 18 V.E.S	
"	8-12-18		5 Horses 1 Mule admitted to the Section	
"	9-12-18		7 Horses 2 Mules admitted to the Section	
"	10-12-18		4 Horses admitted to the Section	
"	10-12-18		15 Horses 4 Mules evacuated to No 18 V.E.S	

Army Form C. 2118.

WAR DIARY
or
INTELLIGENCE SUMMARY.
(Erase heading not required.)

Instructions regarding War Diaries and Intelligence Summaries are contained in F. S. Regs., Part II. and the Staff Manual respectively. Title pages will be prepared in manuscript.

Place	Date	Hour	Summary of Events and Information	Remarks and references to Appendices
In the Field	12-12-18		4 Horses admitted to the Section	
	14-12-18		Major-General N.J.G. Cameron. C.B. Commanding 49(WR) Division visited and inspected the Section	
	14-12-18		2 Horses admitted to the Section	
	15-12-18		1 Horse admitted to the Section	
	16-12-18		Section attended Divisional Ceremonial Parade taken by Lieut-General Sir J. A. Godley K.C.B. Commanding XXII Corps	
	16-17-18		7 Horses admitted to the Section	
	17-12-18		1 Horse admitted to the Section	
	18-12-18		2 Horses admitted to the Section	
	18-12-18		15 Horses 2 Mules evacuated to No 18 V.E.S.	
	19-12-18		3 Horses admitted to the Section	
	20-12-18		2 Horses admitted to the Section	
	20-12-18		No SE 5295 Sergt. F V Redman proceeded on leave to England, leave granted from 21-12-18 to 4-1-19	
	21-12-18		4 Horses admitted to the Section	

Army Form C. 2118.

WAR DIARY
or
INTELLIGENCE SUMMARY.
(Erase heading not required.)

Instructions regarding War Diaries and Intelligence Summaries are contained in F. S. Regs., Part II. and the Staff Manual respectively. Title pages will be prepared in manuscript.

Place	Date	Hour	Summary of Events and Information	Remarks and references to Appendices
In the Field	21-12-18		No. SE 48114 Private S Whitaker RAVC reported for duty from No 2 Veterinary Hospital.	
In the Field	22-12-18		12 Horses / Mule admitted to the Section	
"	23-12-18		3 Horses admitted to the Section	
"	23-12-18		21 Horses 2 Mules evacuated to No 18 VES.	
"	24-12-18		20 Horses admitted to the Section	
"	27-12-18		2 Horses admitted to the Section	
"	26-12-18		21 Horses / Mule evacuated to No 18 VES	
"	28-12-18		No 6E 5234 Private W to Wright RAVC deputated to No 2 Veterinary Hospital Dunfum to Establishment.	
"	28-12-18		3 Horses admitted to the Section	
"	29-12-18		No. T0731 Pte S G Bearsman RAVC proceeded on leave to England, leave granted from 30-12-18 to 13-1-19.	
"	29-12-18		4 Horses / Mule admitted to the Section	
"	30-12-18		14 Horses / Mule admitted to the Section	
"	30-12-18		14 Horses evacuated to No 18 VES.	
"	31-12-18		11 Horses admitted to the Section	
"	3-12-18		20 Horses evacuated to No 18 VES	

Steen
CAPTAIN A. V. C
No. 2? W.S. MOBILE VETERINARY SECTION.

Vol II

War Diary
49th Bn M.G. Corps
January 1919

26
49

WAR DIARY
or
INTELLIGENCE SUMMARY.

Army Form C. 2118.

(Erase heading not required.)

No 8 Vety Sec

Place	Date	Hour	Summary of Events and Information	Remarks and references to Appendices
In the Field	1-1-19		3 Horses 1 Mule admitted to the Section	CAPTAIN, A. V. D. S., & W. R. MOBILE VETERINARY SECTION.
"	2-1-19		1 Horse admitted to the Section	
"	2-1-19		9 Horses 2 Mules evacuated to No 18 V.E.S.	
"	3-1-19		18 Horses admitted to the Section	
"	3-1-19		2 Horses collected by the Motor Ambulance from No 18 V.E.S.	
"	4-1-19		27 Horses admitted to the Section	
"	4-1-19		21 Horses evacuated to No 18 V.E.S.	
"	5-1-19		10 Horses 1 Mule admitted to the Section	
"	5-1-19		27 Horses evacuated to No 18 V.E.S.	
"	6-1-19		20 Horses admitted to the Section	
"	7-1-19		19 Horses 3 Mules admitted to the Section	
"	7-1-19		30 Horses 1 Mule evacuated to No 18 V.E.S.	
"	8-1-19		11 Horses admitted to the Section	
"	9-1-19		10 Horses admitted to the Section	
"	10-1-19		2 Horses admitted to the Section	
"	11-1-19		2 Horses admitted to the Section	

WAR DIARY
or
INTELLIGENCE SUMMARY.

Army Form C. 2118.

Place	Date	Hour	Summary of Events and Information	Remarks and references to Appendices
In the Field	11-1-19		SE 5295. Sergt. F.V Redman RAVC (Demobilized) proceeded to Concentration Camp for dispersal. Strength of this Section brought to unit effective from 11-1-19.	B.E.F. 41 M.M.R MOBILE VETERINARY SECTION. REMAIN, A.V.D.
	13-1-19		(NoSE 6536 Private T. Partridge RAVC admitted 1/3 WR Field Ambulance	
	16-1-19		4 Horses admitted to the Section	
	16-1-19		32 Horses evacuated to No. 18 V.E.S.	
	17-1-19		16 Horses 5 Mules evacuated to No. 18 V.E.S.	
	15-1-19		The 5 Brood Mares of Units in this Division admitted to the Section, and were evacuated to No. 18 V.E.S. on 16-1-19	
	18-1-19		24 Horses admitted to the Section	
	19-1-19		3 Horses admitted to the Section	
	20-1-19		8 Horses admitted to the Section	
	20-1-19		14 Horses 1 Mule evacuated to No. 18 V.E.S.	
	21-1-19		2 Horses admitted to the Section	
	21-1-19		10 Horses evacuated to No. 18 V.E.S.	
	22-1-19		4 Horses 2 Mules admitted to the Section	
	22-1-19		4 Horses discharged to duty to D/245 WR Bde RFA	

Army Form C. 2118.

WAR DIARY
or
INTELLIGENCE SUMMARY

(Erase heading not required.)

Instructions regarding War Diaries and Intelligence Summaries are contained in F.S. Regs., Part II. and the Staff Manual respectively. Title Pages will be prepared in manuscript.

Place	Date	Hour	Summary of Events and Information	Remarks and references to Appendices
In the Field	23-1-19		2 Horses admitted to this Section	
	24-1-19		5 Horses admitted to this Section	
	25-1-19		4 Horses 1 Mule evacuated to No 18 V.E.S.	
	27-1-19		2 Horses 1 Mule admitted to this Section	
	28-1-19		3 Horses admitted to this Section	
	29-1-19		5 Horses admitted to this Section	
	30-1-19		3 Horses admitted to this Section	
	30-1-19		5 Horses evacuated to No 18 V.E.S	
	30-1-19		In accordance with instructions received from SADVS 49 (WR) Division No SE 4814 Pte S WHITAKER RAVC was despatched to First Army Animal Collecting Camp for duty.	
	31-1-19		10 Horses 6 Mules admitted to this Section	

[signature]
B. ---, Captain, R.A.V.C.
1/1 W.R. MOBILE VETERINARY SECTION.

31 Apl 45

War Diary
of
1/1 (WR) M.V.S.
for
the month of February
1919

WAR DIARY or INTELLIGENCE SUMMARY

Army Form C. 2118.

(Erase heading not required.)

Instructions regarding War Diaries and Intelligence Summaries are contained in F. S. Regs., Part II. and the Staff Manual respectively. Title pages will be prepared in manuscript.

Place	Date	Hour	Summary of Events and Information	Remarks and references to Appendices
Nieuwey	1st		Two D. horses admitted for surgical twitching	
	2nd		1 horse sent to ADVS by motor to be destroyed	
			Sent Bombardier Joseph to hospital to be exchanged to D.A.D.C. by motor lorry on leave. Reported a case of suspected epizootic lymphangitis. The subject being mare Army horse recently purchased of Cuban	
	3rd		Capt T Pollard R.A.V.C. O.C. M.V.S. proceeded to Dapham	
			1 - D. animals	
			2 -	
			4 horses admitted. 1 horse evacuated to 18 V.E.S.	
	4th		Sent D. animals (6 horses & 1 mule) field to 97m. M.V.S. at	
	5th		2 horses admitted. 37443 Sergt R.S. Porter R.A.V.C. reported for duty	
	6th		1 horse admitted. Corpl L Fitch R.A.V.C. proceeded on leave to U.K.	
	7th		2 horses & 2 mules admitted to M.V.S.	
	8th		2 horses admitted	
	9th		2 horses admitted	
	10th		1 horse admitted. One D. animal sent to M.V.S. Furnes	
	11th		10 horses evacuated to 18 V.E.S. — G. D. Arnold — 14th regt mule #26	
	12th		Capt T Pollard R.A.V.C. returned from leave	

WAR DIARY
or
INTELLIGENCE SUMMARY
(Erase heading not required.)

Army Form C. 2118.

Place	Date	Hour	Summary of Events and Information	Remarks and references to Appendices
February 14	a		1 Horse Whale adm Sick	
	15		2 S.D. Ambulance from officer commanding 6th Cavalry ref. conf. of proposition for formation of a month calculation from each Brigade to consist	
	16			
	17		Pte S. Mitchell R.A.V.C. proceeded to U.K. 1 Horse adm Sick	
			3 D Horses trek to Mont Fontaine 1 D Hmastel to M. Magulette	
	18		13 Horses adm Sick 3 D ambulance moved to 107 Margit	
	19		2 D Horses trek to M. Mobille	
			1 Horse adm Sick 12 Horses 2 mules removed Sick V.E.S.	
	20		Capt J. POLLARD R.A.V.C. returned from leave - resumed Command S.S.W. THOMAS V.S. Proceeded on leave S.B.	
	21		3 Horses 1 Mule adm Sick	
	22		1 Horse adm Sick	
	23		1 Horse adm Sick S/S 133041 S.S.W. BELSHAM and SE/9511 P Le R.E.	
			HARDSTAFF Joined unit to 49th Div Cavalry Corps to divisional 103171 Sgt. P.S. Symington proceeded U.K. to Hospital Sick 3 Horses Evacuated	
	24		3 Horses Evacuated	
	25			
	26		9 Horses adm Sick 3 D Horses trek to M. Margit	
	27		3 Horses adm Sick	
			4 D Horses 1 Mule adm Sick M.R. Brys admitted 2 D Horses trek to Mobr Forting	
	28		6 Horses 1 mule admitted 6 Horses Evacuated VES	

H.Q.
49 Div'

Herewith War Diary of 4th W.R. M.V.S
for the month of March 1919.
Please acknowledge receipt.

Captain, A.V.C.
B.S./119 W.R. Mobile Veterinary Section.

WAR DIARY
or
INTELLIGENCE SUMMARY
(Erase heading not required.)

Army Form C. 2118.

1/1 W.R. Mob Vety Sec

WE 46

Place	Date	Hour	Summary of Events and Information	Remarks and references to Appendices
In the Field	1-3-19		One Horse 3 Mules admitted to Section	
	2-3-19		5 Horses 1 Mule admitted to Section	
	2-3-19		2 Horses 1 Mule evacuated to No 18 V.E.S	
	2-3-19		TT03285 Sergeant M Ross attached 2/4/6 Bde R.F.A proceeded to Concentration Camp. (for Demobilisation)	
	3-3-19		TT03184 Sergt. H. Singleton A/H, D 2/4/5 Bde R.F.A proceeded to Concentration Camp for Demobilisation	
	4-3-19		2 Horses admitted to Section	
	5-3-19		8 Horses 4 Mules admitted to Section	
	6-3-19		2 Horses evacuated to No 18 V.E.S	
	5-3-19		2 Horses 1 Mule destroyed "Class D"	
	6-3-19		3 Horses admitted to Section	
	6-3-19		5 Horses 1 Mule destroyed "Class D"	
	7-3-19		4 Horses 1 Mule admitted to Section	
	7-8-19		4 Horses evacuated to 18 V.E.S	
	7-3-19		7 Horses Mules destroyed "Class D"	
	7-3-19		32 Horses 5 Mules were sold by Public Auction by M. Defroy Notaire a Douai at the Chateau Bisancourt at road to Warendin	
	9-3-19		3 Horses admitted to Section	
	10-3-19		3 Horses admitted to Section	
	10-3-19		5 Horses 1 Mule Destroyed "Class D"	
	10-3-19		ST. 3602 Sergt. B.H. Eggleton A/H B 2/4/5 Bde R.F.A proceeded to Concentration Camp for Demobilisation	
	10-3-19		TT03166 L/Sgt D. Greenwood A/H C 2/4/5 Bde R.F.A. proceeded to concentration camp for Demobilisation	
	11-3-19		2 Horses 5 Mules admitted to Section	
	12-3-19		23 Horses 28 Mules admitted to Section	

WAR DIARY or INTELLIGENCE SUMMARY

Army Form C. 2118.

Place	Date	Hour	Summary of Events and Information	Remarks and references to Appendices
In the Field	12-3-19		5 Horses 6 Mules evacuated to No 18 V.E.S	
	13-3-19		3 Horses 2 Mules admitted to the Section	
	13-3-19		4 Horses "Glass D" destroyed	
	14-3-19		3 Mules evacuated to No 8 V.E.S	
	14-3-19		8 Horses 21 Mules evacuated to No 18 V.E.S	
	14-3-19		6 Horses 1 Mule "Glass D" destroyed	
	14-3-19		TTO 3215 Sergt. A.A. Huckaby a/H 148 Inf. Bde. proceeded to concentration camp for Demobilisation	
	15-3-19		S/E 7120 Sergt. W.J. Edwards a/H. C 246 Bn.A.Y.F.A. proceeded to concentration camp for Demobilisation	
	15-3-19		40 Animals sold by Public Auction by M. Defany Notair a Donai at the Chateau Barincourt Roost Wanenelin	
	16-3-19		4 Horses 4 Mules admitted to the Section	
	17-3-19		6 Horses 2 Mules admitted to the Section	
	17-3-19		5 Horses 15 Mules Evacuated to No 18 V.E.S	
	17-3-19		7 Horses 2 Mules Destroyed "Glass D"	
	17-3-19		TTO 3189 Sergt. J Hopkin S/H 147 Inf. Bde. proceeded to concentration camp for Demobilisation	
	19-3-19		1 Mule admitted to Section	
	19-3-19		7 Horses 3 Mules (Glass D) destroyed	
	20-3-19		1 Horse 3 Mules admitted to the Section	
	20-3-19		2 Horses Evacuated to No 18 V.E.S	
	22-3-19		5 Horses admitted to the Section	
	22-3-19		4 Horses 3 Mules evacuated to No 18 V.E.S	
	25-3-19		2 Mules admitted to the Section	

CAPTAIN, A.V.C.
O.C. W.R. MOBILE VETERINARY SECTION

WAR DIARY
or
INTELLIGENCE SUMMARY

Army Form C. 2118.

Place	Date	Hour	Summary of Events and Information	Remarks and references to Appendices
In the Field	26-3-19		10 Horses & 6 Mules sold by Public Auction by M. Dupuy, Notaire a Douai, at the Station Bernicourt Road Waranchin	
	27-3-19		Section Evacuated Billets at Chaloin Bernicourt and moved to the Artillery Barracks, Douai.	
	27-3-19		2 Horses Class D admitted to the Section	
	27-3-19		1 Mule evacuated to No 18 V.E.S	
	28-3-19		2 Horses Class D admitted to the Section	

J.B.C.
Captain, A.V.C.
1/1 W.R. Mobile Veterinary Section

www.ingramcontent.com/pod-product-compliance
Lightning Source LLC
Chambersburg PA
CBHW080846230426
43662CB00013B/2036